Ambassador Ortiz

Ambassador Ortiz

Lessons from a Life of Service

Ambassador Frank V. Ortiz

Edited by
Don J. Usner

UNIVERSITY OF NEW MEXICO PRESS ❖ ALBUQUERQUE

Dedication

To Catherine,
who saw value in this telling.

To Dolores,
who gave the telling its value.

Published 2005
10 09 08 07 06 05 1 2 3 4 5 6

Library of Congress Cataloging-in-Publication Data

Ortiz, Frank V., 1926–
Ambassador Ortiz : lessons from a life of service / Frank V. Ortiz;
edited by Don J. Usner.
p. cm.
ISBN 0-8263-3712-0 (Cloth : alk. paper)
1. Ortiz, Frank V., 1926– 2. Ambassadors—United States—Biography.
I. Usner, Donald J. II. Title.
E840.8.078A3 2005
327.73'0092—dc22

2004023087

Design and composition by Melissa Tandysh

Frontispiece: Official photo of Ambassador Ortiz

Contents

Introduction by Governor Bill Richardson
vii

Prologue
1

CHAPTER 1. Origins in Santa Fe
4

CHAPTER 2. Out Into the World:
Washington Politics and Wartime Horror
21

CHAPTER 3. Into America's Front Line Trenches:
Passing the Exams and a Special Mission to the Sudan
36

CHAPTER 4. Reassignment Ethiopia:
At the Emperor's Court and Following in Burton's Footsteps
46

CHAPTER 5. Mexico City the First Time Around:
A Prideful Mistake
64

CHAPTER 6. In the Heart of the State Department
71

CHAPTER 7. Mexico for a Second Time:
A Successful Negotiation
77

CHAPTER 8. A Time of Transition in Spain—
Department of State
86

CHAPTER 9. Peru:
A Bizarre Accusation
95

CHAPTER 10. Uruguay:
Living with Terror
105

CHAPTER 11. Back to the Home Office:
The Southern Cone and Working with Kissinger
111

CHAPTER 12. Barbados and the Caribbean:
Reaching the Top Rungs of the Ladder
116

CHAPTER 13. Guatemala:
The Failure of a Mission
125

CHAPTER 14. Panama to Peru:
A Tropical Interlude and a Contentious Return
143

CHAPTER 15. Argentina:
The Pinnacle of a Career
158

CHAPTER 16. Home at Last—
But Not for Long
180

CHAPTER 17. Home to Stay:
More Lessons to Learn
188

Postscript
205

Introduction

GOVERNOR BILL RICHARDSON OF NEW MEXICO

I first met Ambassador Ortiz in 1974, just after my graduation from the Fletcher School of Tufts University and had begun work in the Congressional Relations Office of the Department of State in Washington. Ambassador Ortiz had recently returned from three difficult years of service in the American Embassy in Montevideo, Uruguay. During those critical years democratic Uruguay was under attack by one of the most dangerous terrorist threats our Americas have known. That threat was overcome and Uruguay continues on its democratic way. In those early years Ambassador Ortiz and I were drawn together by our shared dedication to creating a hemisphere in which our southern neighbors enjoyed the blessings of a free exercise of political and economic choices and the rule of law that democracy brings. We joined with many others working towards that long-desired goal. Twelve years later, in 1986, with all of Latin America except for Cuba led by democratically elected governments, that dream was closer than ever before to being realized. Our common efforts towards that shared goal bonded the two of us as we continued our lifetimes of public service.

As a representative of New Mexico in the national congress in 1985 I visited Ambassador Ortiz in Buenos Aires, where he was serving as the American Ambassador. There we rejoiced together in Argentina's return to democracy after a long, dark period of terror and dictatorship.

We next had contact in the national congress in Washington, when Ambassador Ortiz came to remind me that New Mexico's unequalled historic patrimony was in imminent danger of being lost. He made a compelling case for the urgent construction of a modern facility in which New Mexico's irreplaceable treasures could be safely stored, conserved, and above all, exhibited to inspire future generations. He urged me to help obtain federal funds, without which the new museum could not be built. Obtaining those and other funds took many years and much hard work by many. Those efforts were successful. As Governor of New Mexico in 2004, I had the pleasure of authorizing the appropriation by the State Legislature of the final balance to match the federal funds that had been obtained. The collaboration between Ambassador Ortiz and me that began thirty years ago has resulted in beginning the construction of a new museum worthy of New Mexico's history.

Ambassador Ortiz's autobiography, to which I contribute these lines, is another collaboration in which we share a commitment to the coming generations by inspiring them to reach for the stars. In writing his autobiography, Ambassador Ortiz, an "ordinary but curious kid from Santa Fe," as he would have it, tells us how he made that stretch. We have faith that our joint aspirations will again be fulfilled as new generations rise to the challenges our world presents.

Prologue

One of the few advantages of reaching an advanced age is that one knows not only the beginnings of stories, but also their middles and, most times, how they end. This knowledge brings a sense of completion. One can reflect on the lessons that life's experiences teach. Such is the vantage I enjoy as I reflect on some of the extraordinary events of my life.

The world's libraries are filled with books by authors from remote towns who went out into wider worlds, learned from their experiences, and decided to share what they learned. Reflecting on my own life and career in the American Foreign Service, I similarly decided to record its lessons. I hope that by doing so, young people—especially young New Mexican Hispanics—may be inspired to stretch their expectations. The success that innate advantages, luck, and hard work brought to me is still out there for those who will seek it.

Something I realized early in my long time away from New Mexico is that, simply by virtue of being born and raised there, I was blessed with gifts that served me greatly in my career and personal life. I believe that New Mexicans generally share these advantages. Many are not aware of that fact, but with a little reflection, it is obvious. New Mexicans represent a community of survivors. Our ancestors spent many of the past 400 years in near-total isolation in a very harsh environment. After traveling thousands of miles across menacing terrain and punishing climates, our ancestors—men women, and children—put down deep roots in these little valleys. They had to endure great poverty, abandonment, and hostility from others. From the 500 original Spanish colonists of 1598, the number of Hispanic New Mexicans has grown to over 500,000. We come from tough, vigorous stock. We are not weaklings.

A primary asset that has brought Hispanic New Mexicans cohesively this far is a deep religious faith. We generally accept that there is a grand scheme to life, where both good and evil exist. We share the conviction that something cannot come from nothing, so that somewhere, sometime, there had to be a generative act of creation, which we choose to personalize. We further personalize many other aspects of our religious observances. Throughout our lifetimes we are accompanied by a legion of companions whose saintly lives inspire us to resolve life's challenges. The traditional New Mexican is never lonely. This comforting cadre of allies and a deep faith elevate the spirit and give the strength to overcome difficulties. That has certainly been my experience and I believe I share it with many, if not most, Hispanic New Mexicans.

Another advantage is that Hispanic New Mexicans come from a tolerant and courteous culture. Cultural diversity has been the norm in northern New Mexico for a very long time. Survival has demanded that diverse cultural groups interact with each other peacefully. Being the "in-your-face" type would not have served our ancestors well, so they learned to accept one another, and they passed along that ability. As a consequence, New Mexicans are less unnerved when they encounter different peoples and cultures elsewhere in the world. That's an advantage lacking in individuals growing up in more culturally homogenous places.

Instinctively I have relied on this ability to accommodate different kinds of people and their customs. My first week in the Near East Office of the State Department, for example, I was sent to ceremonially escort the Egyptian Ambassador to call on Secretary of State Atcheson. Being a fellow dry-gulcher and friendly, I extended my right hand to the Ambassador. He took it and firmly passed it to his left hand. Then hand in hand, as Arab men will do, we walked through the lobby up the elevator and down the hallways. The Egyptian Ambassador only turned loose of my hand when we reached the Secretary's office. Some of those in the building gave us startled or amused looks. This experience may have unnerved some, but it didn't faze me. I simply took it as a novel learning experience.

In the Foreign Service, one must be prepared for many such experiences. In four decades in the foreign service, I withstood—without flinching—from male professional contacts kisses on both cheeks and the mouth (from Arabs and Slavs); a thorough kneading of my back, neck and bicep muscles (from Mexicans); rib-cracking embraces (most Latins); iron-grip or dead-fish handshakes (universal); and timid pats on the head (from various cultures).

The only time my wife, Dolores, intervened to break this proud record of multicultural adaptation was in Ethiopia, when we innocently agreed to be witnesses at a friend's wedding. At the marriage feast we were led into a richly decorated bridal chamber to serve as formal witnesses to the actual consummation of the marriage. Dolores dragged me out of there, though I protested that we were obliged to comply with our duties—which would have included parading probative bed linens among the guests.

So often when people talk about New Mexico, they speak of the state's weaknesses and deficiencies. I want to turn that notion around. I want to emphasize the strengths of this marvelous place and its people. I believe that my upbringing in a Hispanic family in Santa Fe helped me very much in rising to the top of the diplomatic service—a very competitive profession. These cultural assets proved so strong that they opened many doors for me, an ordinary but curious kid from Santa Fe. I record here my own true story as testament to this fact and as an encouragement to others like me.

By doing so, I echo Bernal Diaz del Castillo, who wrote, "It is my fortune to have no other wealth to leave my sons and descendents except this, my true story, and they will see what a wonderful one it is."

1

Origins in Santa Fe

Political turmoil and armed violence came into my life before I was two years old. I cannot recall that dramatic event, when my mother and I hugged the floor of a train to dodge bullets as we escaped Mexico City during the Cristero Revolt. That experience presaged what I would sometimes face during my four-decade career in the American Foreign Service, when my official duties placed me in close contact with great world leaders and tyrants and made me a target for terrorist militants and political activists. More than once I found myself in the middle of the overthrow of governments by elements as determined as the Cristeros.

I was born in the old St. Vincent hospital on March 14, 1926, into a family whose various branches have lived in Santa Fe since its settlement in 1607. At the time my father, Frank Valencia Ortiz y Barbero, and mother, Margarita Delgado y García, were living in Mexico City. My father represented an American watch company. He sold watches and clocks in Mexico, the Caribbean, and Central America. It was a very good job.

When he first had word that he had a position with the watch company, my father's mother, doña Alcaria—a very orthodox, old school Spanish matriarch—did not approve of her son leaving New Mexico to go live among Protestants. The company had sent him his train tickets and an advance of money to travel to Connecticut for training. When he woke to catch the train, however, he found that doña Alcaria had taken all his clothes, hidden his money, and left the house. Fortunately for him, she overlooked his train tickets. So he left his home in spite of his mother's efforts to keep him there.

My father was a very determined man. He was resolute that he would take that job, and he overcame all obstacles in his way. He walked barefoot and in his underclothes to the neighbor's house to borrow trousers and a shirt. He couldn't find shoes that fit, but relatives loaned him a few dollars and he made it to the train on time. When he arrived in New York the company advanced money so he could dress himself properly. I didn't face such hurdles at the start of my career—my parents encouraged me to aim for the stars—but I do think I inherited some of my father's determination.

From Mexico City, my mother traveled home to New Mexico so I would be born in Santa Fe, as was the family tradition. She returned with me to Mexico City when I was still a wee baby. We lived on Calle Lopez, which is very close to the Palace of Fine Arts. Interestingly enough, my ancestors—particularly on Mother's side—had been traders over both the Chihuahua and Santa Fe trails. Their frequent travels to Mexico had forged a family history and connection with Mexico. (My children have maintained that connection.)

I was one year old in 1927 when the Cristero Revolt erupted in Mexico with renewed violence. The Cristeros were Catholics who rebelled because of severe persecution. When their forces attacked Mexico City, the situation became so dangerous that my father put Mother and me on a train for San Antonio, Texas—one of the last trains to leave the city. Mother said we had to lay on the floor to dodge bullets sailing through the train windows.

We arrived in San Antonio when I was about a year and a half. Soon afterwards, the big crash of 1929 hit and few people were buying watches or any other luxury items. My father lost his job, so we came back to Santa Fe and settled in a house on de Vargas Street. I began school in 1931 and was educated in the Santa Fe Public Schools through high school, finishing in 1943.

In those days the schools of Santa Fe were very good and I had an excellent education. Teachers were strict, formal, and very well trained. Many suffered from respiratory ailments and had come from the Midwest or New England to New Mexico for the dry climate. My parents started me in school early, when I was five-and-one-half years old, which was a problem for me. I was almost two years younger than most of the kids in my class. I was always the littlest guy—the one who got body hair later than anyone else and the last one to have my voice change. The fellows would tease me, saying, "You talk like a girl," and they'd tell jokes that I didn't get at all. I had to work hard to fit in, but still made lots of friends.

I probably should have been placed in a class or two lower, but I strove to keep up with the older kids. I think that was good tempering. It cultivated tenacity. Classmates sometimes picked on me, but that turned out to be a good thing. I had to try hard to keep up and to tolerate harassment.

I had the great fortune of being placed in the "college track." The schools could never do now what they did then in the '30s. Then students took an IQ test and were placed in different educational tracks, depending on their scores. A high score on the test would place a student in a fast track with others deemed capable of university work. Those who didn't do so well on the test were placed in other tracks, with the lowest track designated for those who would go to the vocational school to learn to be carpenters, mechanics, or plumbers. Those kids probably earned much more money than the kids in the college track!

I was put into the fast track and drilled in English grammar, Latin, geography, and advanced math. I graduated in May, 1943 in the Honor Society and received a scholarship to the University of New Mexico, which I didn't take. I also passed the exam for entry into the Naval Academy, but I was too young to attend.

I remember a couple of teachers that made a real difference in my life. One of them was my fifth grade teacher, Mrs. Cox. As I say, I was younger than the other guys and small for my class. I was also very skinny and my ears stuck way out. But Mrs. Cox encouraged me. If I'd do a good paper, she'd praise me in front of the class. I remember once using the word "depopulate" in a paper about sharks. Mrs. Cox thought it was wonderful that a kid of my age would know such a word. She embarrassed me in front of the whole class, telling them how smart I was.

Teachers were very important to me, but I had other mentors as well. Father Jerome, a Franciscan priest in our parish, was Central Casting's version of a Franciscan saint: small, ruddy faced, sweet, and kind. Father Jerome helped me through a difficult time in my life. It is an intimate detail of my personal life, but it was a very important lesson.

Grandmother Alcaria would make sure that I went to mass every holy day and every Sunday. (She impressed this so deeply upon me that I haven't missed more than five or six Sunday masses in my long life!) She made sure that I never crossed my legs in church—she'd pinch me if I did—and that I went to confession and communion. She was vigilant in seeing that I observed all the rites of our church.

When I was about 13 she noticed that I was not going to the communion rail. She asked if I had been to confession. I wanted to lie but I couldn't because I was totally under her domination. So I admitted that I hadn't been for awhile. She said, "Next Saturday you're going," and the next week she escorted me to the confessional.

My confessor, thank heavens, was Father Jerome. I confessed that I was doing things that were really sinful and that I knew that doing them would doom me, but I couldn't seem to help it. I asked him what I should do. Could he grant me absolution? Father Jerome answered by saying, "This is an important time for you. You are being prepared for your life as a man. These are steps towards becoming a real man and, someday, a good father. It is very normal. You don't have to do any penance. Don't worry about it."

That was wonderful news! I came bouncing out of the confessional and there was my grandmother, ready to have me go up to the altar and do a lengthy penance. She asked, "Were you given absolution? Don't you have to do penance?" And I said, "No, no, I am absolved." She never knew what had transpired. It was a very important lesson for me on my path of growing up. I have seldom been burdened with self-induced guilt. (Remorse over my role in bombing Japan during World War II, however, was a big exception.)

My parents always believed in me and encouraged me to get a good education. My father graduated from St. Michael's high school but he never went to college. Nevertheless, his hard-driving personality assured that he usually got his way, schooling or no schooling. My mother was educated at the Loretto Academy and also did not go on to college. She was a very cultivated person. She loved books and music and was one of the great town beauties. She was also extremely artistic, although she had no formal training. A rich art collector once tried to buy one especially fine painting of hers from me. I would never sell that painting.

My mom worked outside the home. She first was employed by the state in secretarial positions, then was elected County Clerk. Her name is on the plaque at the court house. She did wonderful things for me. She brought home reference books, books on Greek mythology, and one about the sinking of the Titanic. I read these and many other great books out at the ranch in the summer.

I was very fortunate to have a very happy childhood with nurturing parents who challenged me and encouraged me to read. I loved to read travel books and also became an avid stamp collector. My father believed in physical labor. He put me in the fields to clear the rocks and prune and irrigate the fruit trees at our ranch above Chupadero. In Santa Fe I had a job on Saturdays at Ballard's grocery store. I was paid a dollar for a day's work—and it was hard work. I took care of all the vegetables, filled orders over the telephone, and delivered them.

I got the job at Ballard's to prove a point to my father. Any time I'd ask my father for money, he would make it a very humiliating experience for me. So one day I got into a thirteen-year-old snit and said, "From now on, I'm not going to ask you for a penny!" He laughed and said, "Well, that'll last until tomorrow."

I went out and found the job at Ballard's Grocery and after that landed a job at the Rancho del Monte dude ranch, where I was a stable boy and maintained the tennis court and watered the gardens. When the cowboys couldn't do it, I'd take horseback riders out on the trail because I knew the area well, since it was in the backyard of our Chupadero summer home. I earned fairly good money during the summer at Rancho del Monte. I lived in the bunkhouse, and I saved what I earned. I made good on my threat not to ask for money from my father. From age thirteen on, I never asked him for another penny.

I'm glad to have grown up in Santa Fe, and, as everyone who knows me will attest, I'm totally devoted to this city. I tell my kids and my family that the dust they breathe probably carries specks of our ancestors. The Delgados, which is my mother's family name, came here in the 1700s—relatively late, compared to other ancestors. On my mother's side I also have two grandmothers with the surname García. On my father's side, the Baca name came very early, with the first Spanish colonists in 1598. The Romeros, the Valencias, the Pachecos, the Ortizes, the Barberos—other names on my father's side—were also among the early colonists. According to family records I am a thirteenth generation New Mexican. Almost all my ancestors were born in Santa Fe, so my historical connection to the city runs very deep. My extended family is large and we are proud of our heritage. Most are still in Santa Fe. We have a sense of place and family. I think this is one of the most valuable things that our culture here gave me. Young independence-minded people today may not appreciate the value of a large, close family, but it's a real strength and it's still here. Having extended family close by is especially valuable if there's trouble. Then it really helps.

When I was working at the U.S. embassy in Mexico City, about one-fourth of the population of the city made just barely enough money to get through each day. They had to share in order to survive. A little boy in the family would shine shoes, the mother would clean houses, the father would fix plumbing, the oldest boy would sell newspapers, and the grandmother would sell flowers. They pooled their earnings and together they could exist and feel sheltered. That kept Mexico together in my time. A similar sense of family and community was also very important in New Mexico in the early days. It kept people together through all the hard times of the past four centuries.

I grew up in a bilingual household, speaking the archaic Spanish characteristic of northern New Mexico. We knew our Spanish was different, so later my parents sent me to Spain, to the Complutense University in Madrid, to learn the King's Spanish, so to speak. That was in 1950, after I graduated from Georgetown University School of Foreign Service.

My family has always had a sense of civic responsibility. An early record of this is my great-grandfather Felipe Delgado's presidential commission, signed by Abraham Lincoln in April of 1865, shortly before Lincoln was assassinated. Don Felipe served as Superintendent of Indian Affairs for the New Mexico Territory. He earned this position during the Civil War, when the Confederates invaded New Mexico in an attempt to secure a route to the Colorado gold mines and to California. It was very important to the Union to stop the Confederates from succeeding.

When the Confederates marched into southern New Mexico, the Union army was concerned about the role that the Indians would play in the coming conflict. Don Felipe came up with a successful way to secure the Indians' loyalty to the Union cause. He recommended that President Lincoln send to New Mexico silver-headed canes bearing symbols of the United States government. The canes would be given to the pueblo governors from the Great White Father, thus bestowing upon them a *bastón de mando*. Don Felipe predicted that the governors would feel recognized and valued as leaders and would remain loyal to Lincoln.

The canes also symbolized the sovereignty of the pueblos. The Spanish crown, through the colonial governors, were the first to present canes of authority to the pueblos, back in the eighteenth century. It was a way of cementing alliances and recognizing the authority of the pueblo leaders—a symbolic act that kings of Spain had used for centuries to secure loyalty. In suggesting that Lincoln send canes, don Felipe repeated a ritual his ancestors had used successfully before. To this day some of the pueblos still have those Lincoln canes.

The Union army engaged the invading Confederates in two important battles, the decisive one taking place at Glorieta. Throughout the hostilities, the Confederates found no significant support among Hispanics or the Pueblos. At Glorieta, the invaders' supply trains were burned and the Confederates retreated to Texas. Before Lincoln was assassinated, he acknowledged don Felipe's role in securing the Indians' support by giving him the commission. Lincoln also sent as gifts to don Felipe an elegant gold pen and a fine Brady photograph. (The photograph was later stolen from our ranch.)

I emulated don Felipe's actions when King Juan Carlos visited New Mexico in 1987. Knowing that the King would participate in a ceremony with the Pueblo governors, I recommended that he bring canes of authority to present to the pueblos, and he did just that. Some of the pueblos had lost their original canes from the King of Spain, and they were greatly moved to receive new ones. It was a very touching ceremony. The Indians kissed the canes, made the sign of the cross with them, and were careful not to let them touch the ground. (Governor Bruce King also decided to give the pueblos canes, so the Indians now have plenty of canes!)

From the cradle, my family instilled in me very strong traditions that still govern me. I'm deeply influenced by my heritage. I care a lot about it, and many of the things I do in Santa Fe concern my efforts to preserve and pass on these traditions. I have tried to instill them in my kids. It's rare these days to have a strong familial and traditional connection to the past, particularly in the United States. Great pressures encourage conformity with the dominant culture. Young people especially don't like to be different; they are inclined to blend in with their peers. It is important to carry on with strong traditions like those we have in New Mexico. It's one of the strengths we must maintain.

Somewhat paradoxically, many of my ancestors were very open to change and to outsiders, in spite their strong foundation in tradition. When the American occupation came, for example, relatives on my mother's side chose to collaborate with the Americans because they welcomed the new business opportunities that Americanization would present. The Delgados had been trading on the Santa Fe Trail for years and they were already at ease with Americans. Not all my forefathers shared these sentiments, however. Two priests of the family were probably involved in plotting the Taos revolt in 1847, when the locals tried violently to overthrow American rule, which resulted in much bloodshed, including the assassination of the American governor. That was something of an anomaly in the family.

One of the early heads of the Delgado family, don Manuel Salustiano Delgado, was particularly active in trade via the Santa Fe trail. He and his sons would travel to Missouri and return with items that were scarce and very expensive in New Mexico, like bolts of cloth, nails, hatchets, gunpowder, bullets, and guns, They made good profits off this trade, especially from the big barrels of Kentucky whiskey that they brought back by wagon.

On the way back from one of these trading trips, don Manuel, who was my great-great-grandfather, contracted pneumonia and died. This happened in Kansas, near small towns populated entirely by Protestants. Upon their father's death, the sons reportedly decided they could not bury their father on alien soil. So, one son had an inspiration. He took the top off a whiskey barrel, doubled Papa up, put him in the barrel, and sealed it again. Don Manuel Salustiano was beautifully pickled for the trip home, where he was properly buried.

But that's not the end of the story. In Spanish culture we used the term *malas lenguas*—literally, the "bad tongues"—for people who are critical and envious of others. When don Manuel's sons came back with Papa in the barrel, the malas lenguas began saying that his children had sold the whisky from the barrel. The rumor was that the unsuspecting imbibers proclaimed, "This is the best whiskey you've ever brought back. What body! What flavor!"

There were around ten to twenty thousand people in Santa Fe when I was growing up. I don't remember my parents ever forbidding me to go anywhere. I had total run of the place. It was a small town, but there were always interesting people around, and they were very accessible and friendly with kids. The art community was vibrant. I remember the artist Alfred Morang would often buy a big jug of cheap California sherry and have a salon at his house. Strange, fascinating people would attend. I couldn't drink, but I did sit and listen to what they said. I remember those evenings well. In spite of the isolation of Santa Fe I found stimulation in situations like that.

Santa Fe still had a rural feel to it. The *acequia* system was intact, with the ditches always running full. The area around Acequia Madre, Garcia Street, and Delgado Street was filled with pear and apple trees. The Santa Fe river, too, ran year-round. We used to dam it to make a swimming hole. Once, my brother and I made a dam and were swimming right off the Old Santa Fe Trail. My sister was up above on the bank watching us. We were having a great time when she suddenly began screaming at us, "Get out, get out!" And we did jump out, in a hurry, because we could see she was terrified. Just as we reached the top of the bank, a huge wall of water came down the river. It had been raining in the mountains, creating a powerful wall of water. If my sister hadn't been there watching, I wouldn't be here. My sister's wedding present to me was a painting of that event.

I have one brother, Alfred, and one sister, Adelina, in my immediate family, but of course I was related to practically everybody in town. I was the oldest child in my family. We lived first on de Vargas Street, near the old San Miguel church. Our home was called Placita San Miguel. Now it's a tony bed and breakfast. It is very odd to see it that way. Later we moved to Calle San Pasqual, off Acequia Madre.

There were several distinct neighborhoods in town. The east side kids didn't like the west side kids—a rivalry that still exists. Back then, though, the hostilities were expressed more innocently. We boys made rubber guns by cutting planks in the shape of rifles. We cut little notches along the top of the plank. Then, we'd make thick rubber bands out of old inner tubes and we'd stretch the rubber band back and stick it in a notch. The farther back you pulled the band, the farther it would sail when you released it—and the more it would hurt when it hit the targeted person. Shooting these things at each other is the only violent thing I remember doing. It was sort of dangerous, but nothing compared to what rival kids use on each other now.

When I was growing up I never questioned authority. I behaved myself in school. I didn't smoke or drink, and the one time I strayed seems comical in retrospect. Byron Nesbitt, a fellow student from Española, was my enticer. I was probably fourteen, attending a birthday party at Dr. Brown's residence for his beautiful daughter, Eloisa.

During the party, Byron went into one of the back rooms and sent word out, "Come to the back bedroom." I went to see what was going on. Byron had stolen a bottle of whiskey from his father and was selling long drinks for a quarter. I happened to have a quarter, so I took a good slug. I gagged. It was awful! I've not been keen on alcohol since.

Another adolescent memory that I treasure is the delightful custom of a Sunday night concert on the Plaza by the Conquistadores Band. It seemed that the whole town came to listen to the music, visit, and promenade. As a young adolescent, my grandmother freed me from sitting on a bench with her while she chatted with her *comadres.* I was allowed to join with the boys promenading around the Plaza in one direction, while the girls, arm-in-arm, paraded in the opposite direction. Bold, discreet, and embarrassed glances were exchanged as we passed one another, but I carried the procedure farther. Passing a girl with blue eyes, I'd murmur (or croak, since my voice was changing), "So little blue for so much heaven." For a girl in black I'd say, "Who died in heaven that the angels are mourning?" For a girl in green, I'd offer, "You're delicious when you're green—what will you be like when you're ripe?" The girls, of course, were thrilled and considered me an incipient poet. I never confessed that I learned these *piropos* (flirtatious remarks) from my father, who had used them in Mexico. The girl who really attracted me, Frances Anton, never wore black or green, and she had dark eyes. I could never figure out what to murmur to her.

Those days seem so simple now. Just to smoke was considered really wicked and we knew nothing about drugs. I was awfully lucky to be influenced by good people. I could have been influenced by bad ones. Growing up wasn't always easy for me, but Santa Fe was a very safe, nurturing place, and the protective Spanish culture was very much intact. I can say my childhood was idyllic.

I learned much from our cultural traditions. One of my earliest and most important experiences took place when I was five or six. I was playing with mud when my grandmother doña Alcaria arrived. She took me home, cleaned me up, and dressed me in a white shirt and dark pants. I wondered what we were going to do. She said, "Don

Andrés Constante has died." I only vaguely knew what this meant. She said, "We're going to his *velorio*."

The home where they had don Andrés's wake wasn't too far away. Grandmother brought me there and we entered the large living room. People were sitting in chairs placed around the walls. In the middle of the room, don Andrés was laid out in a coffin with a kneeler in front. I recognized him, but I couldn't quite figure out what this was all about.

A couple of women in the room were wailing, beating their chests and crying, "Oh, the terrible loss!" and other exclamations of grief. They were professional wailers, so to speak—women who the family paid for making a good show of grieving. They caught my attention.

My grandmother brought me up to the coffin and we knelt before it. She said, "Now we're going to pray for don Andrés." For a six-year-old, this wasn't scary. It was just strange. We knelt before don Andrés for a while and then went back and sat at the edge of the room. Many other people came in and did the same thing. Amazingly, in the midst of all this, someone from don Andrés's family called out from the next room, "The food is ready, and the sodas are on the table!" All at once, the wailing stopped. The women who were carrying on stopped just like that and led the procession to the feast.

I vividly remember my grandmother saying to me, "This is very important. I took you away from playing to see don Andrés. Death is going to happen to you. It happens to all of us. It's going to happen to me. And right now you have to know that you will die and that everything you do is in preparation for that. Don't forget this."

I never did forget that experience or my grandmother's words. I remembered it years later, when I was working in Washington. My boss, a wonderful Irish fellow named Jeremiah O'Connor, died very suddenly and his family held a wake at their home. Dolores and I attended. As we approached the body laying in state, Dolores turned to me and said, "Frank, you know, I've never seen a dead person. For me, people pass away; they don't die." This was when she was in her 30s. Very upset, she said, "Why would they do that? Why would they leave the coffin open? I've never seen anybody like this."

Dolores was shocked. But I had become familiar with death and dying at a young age, so death seemed perfectly natural to me. In the Spanish culture in which I was raised, you died—you didn't pass away, "leave," or pass on. I was taught that death is very much a part of life.

The most wonderful part of my life as a kid was my time on the family ranch in the forest above Chupadero. Every year in May we would move to this, the most wonderful place in the world. We had a large house made of stone, that's still standing. It was a dream place. At first, it had no heating or lights. We had to use candles and lamps before we finally got electricity. It was paradise. I grew up climbing mountains there and reveling in a nature wonderland.

We planted about 200 fruit trees at the ranch and we had a cow that provided us with milk. We made our own cheese and butter and put up jams and jellies from the apricot trees. I had a horse named Frenchy. It was a wonderful place for us. It also was good for my parents because during the day, while they were in town working, we were out there running wild, with minimum need for supervision. On the weekends, my parents would invite their friends for lunch. It was my job to kill and pluck the chickens for the Sunday meal. I dispatched the chickens with an axe.

A regular Sunday guest was Dr. José Maldonado. I think it was from my contact with him that I got the idea that I wanted to go to medical school and become a doctor. I thought I would return to live in Santa Fe, make a lot of money, and uphold the family tradition of service. That's what I started out to do with my career—until I had my wartime experience, which changed everything.

While my mother and father both worked in town, Antonia, a woman from the village, cooked and watched out for us. She was too heavy to catch us when we ran from her after being naughty. Antonia's brother Roque was our handyman at the ranch. Antonia made wonderful pies and other delights. Almost every night for dinner she would make Spanish rice, and we would often have beans and *posole*. We made our own flour tortillas and every Sunday we enjoyed a chicken dinner with guests, after the whole family had gone to mass at Saint Francis Cathedral.

We weren't rich by any means. We were middle class, but since someone in the family always held public office of one sort or another, we had this feeling that a lot was expected of us. We behaved in a way that indicated that we had high standards. Some people may have felt we were acting aloof, but our sense of class wasn't based on money.

My family has always been very much a part of the Santa Fe community. All the years I was away, I always had it in my mind that this was my home and that I would return. I never doubted it for a minute. My roots in New Mexico were too deep to permit me to be transplanted anywhere else.

Grandmother doña Alcaria Barbero y Valencia de Ortiz

My mother Margaret Delgado de Ortiz (center)
modeling her grandmother's dress at fiesta time

High school graduate,
Santa Fe, New Mexico, 1943

The ranch house

2

Out Into the World: Washington Politics and Wartime Horror

When I finished high school, I was the youngest boy in my class. All my pals had gone to war. This was in May of 1943. I was just seventeen, too young to enlist, but I desperately wanted to go to war, too. I was a dedicated patriot and felt that I wasn't doing my duty. So I went to the Naval recruiting office and fibbed that I was eighteen years old. I enlisted in the V-12 program and was all set to be sent to Chicago to train for the Navy when my father discovered my ploy and denounced me. The Navy turned me down and I was left miserable, with nothing to do.

Fortunately, my father had contacts in Washington that saved the situation. He was high up in the Democratic party at that time. During his lifetime, he served as chairman of the state Democratic party, a state tax commissioner, and Santa Fe County Clerk. He was a national bituminous coal commissioner and was a close adviser to several New Mexico governors. These public offices allowed him to make important connections.

When the Navy rejected me, my father called New Mexico's Senator Carl Hatch in Washington and asked if he might find a place for me in the senator's staff or elsewhere in the Senate. Senator Hatch offered me a position with the important-sounding title of Liaison Officer of the United States Senate.

Before I left for Washington, my father took me to the First National Bank of Santa Fe and we signed a note for the money for the train fare and my initial stay in Washington until my Senate salary began. I was terrified to be borrowing so much money—as I remember, about $200. To me, that was an awful sum to repay.

Once in Washington, I was so nervous about the loan that I tried to pay it off immediately. Instead of stretching it out, I paid $100 one month and $100 the next month. As a result, I ran very low on money, but I couldn't bring myself to tell my family that I was broke. Instead I chose to live on next to nothing. I ate only twice a day: in the morning, a raw egg in a little glass with tomato juice, and then a liverwurst sandwich and a bowl of bean soup about two in the afternoon. That kept me alive for about two weeks. When I finally told my dad I had paid off the loan in two months he said, "You're crazy! Why did you do that?" He explained to me that a debt is something you pay off over as much time as you can. That was a revelation to me, but I learned the power of credit.

I started my job as Liaison Officer soon after arriving in Washington. I sat on a bench in an ornate little lobby outside the Senate chambers. My job was to take messages in to the senators or call them out for visitors. I ranked just above the page boys, who brought the senators water and cigarettes and other minor things.

The job was a remarkable learning experience. The Senate was a den of lions, where great senators like Vandenberg and Connolly practiced their oratory. I became well acquainted with Prescott Bush, who was a senator from Connecticut, and Senator Truman of Missouri. I found myself involved in high Washington politics at the mere age of seventeen. I was not particularly impressed. I wasn't afraid of the great politicians, and I didn't kowtow to them. I came to feel that it was perfectly normal to deal with legendary and powerful figures. The senators were generally kind to me, and I got along well with most. (Henry Wallace, the Vice President and President of the Senate, was a notable exception. He was a strange person. I knew him well and wasn't comfortable around him.)

One experience during my time in the Senate stands out for me. This was an interaction I had with Senator Robert A. Taft of Ohio, a very cerebral fellow who concentrated on budget figures and was renowned for his opposition to President Roosevelt.

One day an impressive looking man approached me and said, "I'd like to speak with Senator Taft. Would you bring him out?" I said, "Yes, sir, of course. Your name, please?" And he replied "Mr. Baldwin." In those days the senators attended chamber sessions, and I went in to find Senator Taft sitting at his paper-littered desk, half listening to the debate. I told him that a Mr. Baldwin wished to see him. He looked at me and said, "Tell him you can't find me." So I said, "Yes, sir," and went back out and dutifully reported to Mr. Baldwin: "I'm sorry, the Senator is not on the floor. He must have left and I don't know where he's gone." Baldwin drew himself up and said, "Listen, I've just come from the gallery and I saw him on the floor. Would you tell him that Governor Baldwin of Connecticut insists upon seeing him?" I said, "Yes, sir," and went back and told Senator Taft that the man was Governor Baldwin. The senator got up and followed me out of the chamber. As we walked up to the Governor, Taft said, "That stupid boy never can find me."

I was outraged! I wanted to make a fuss but didn't. I talked to my boss, Mr. Perry, who said simply, "That's what you're here for. Don't get upset. That's part of the game." Although humiliated, I had learned an important lesson: in public service, sometimes you must take unfounded criticism. You have to sublimate your own emotions for a greater cause. This proved to be a very valuable lesson for me years later as a diplomat in the Foreign Service dealing with all manner of difficult characters.

The time in the Senate was a great education for me. While working there, I enrolled in night classes at George Washington University. Since I wanted to become a doctor or a dentist and come back home to live in Santa Fe, I concentrated on pre-med courses. I was pledged to Sigma Chi Fraternity, an enviable acceptance that established me on the campus as a person of worth. Those were very good, happy times for me, but I was still determined to go to war. And I did. On the very stroke of my eighteenth birthday, March 14, 1944, I enlisted in the Army Air Force.

My parents were upset, but I was eighteen and they couldn't stop me. If I had to enlist, they said, they wanted me to enter the Navy. But I was unhappy with the way the Navy had previously treated me, so I joined the Army Air Force. My friends and all my schoolmates were already at war. Some of them had been killed.

I went into the service in April and had my basic training in Biloxi, Mississippi. I was there in the summer time and you can't imagine the mosquitoes, dampness, and oppressive heat. I found myself sloughing through the swamps with types of people that I'd never encountered before: tough guys from Brooklyn, Scandinavians from Minnesota, flashy guys from California. It was good for me.

The first thing the trainers did was to give us a pilot aptitude test, to see if we would make good pilots. They put me in a flight simulator and said, "Hold onto this wheel," and then it was just like I was taking off and landing an airplane. This was all new to me. I had never in my life done anything like that. In fact, I'd never even driven a car. So I flunked that test. They said I wouldn't make a good pilot, which didn't bother me a bit.

Instead of flight school they sent me to radio school in Sioux Falls, South Dakota—for the winter. I've never been in a colder place. We lived in rows of tar paper barracks with peaked roofs. For heating, each barrack had a potbelly stove in the middle of the floor. We'd go into Sioux Falls when we had time off. We'd meet girls at the Arkoda ballroom and dance or bowl with them for entertainment. One time I stayed so late that I missed the last bus to the base and I had to walk back in the January cold. My nose hairs froze up and I had to breathe through my mouth and there was frost on my eyebrows. I was lucky I didn't get frostbite. Never had I experienced such cold.

I learned how to be a radio operator that frigid winter. During that time something remarkable happened that gave me a profound lesson in fate. The top students were given a three day pass to Minneapolis before we went overseas. I was hitchhiking back to the base with a fellow from New Jersey named Brickner. A college professor picked us up and while we were driving back to Sioux Falls we got into a discussion about fate. Brickner was saying that nothing could happen until it was ordained. He believed that everything was predetermined by fate. During this high-level discussion I began making fun of Brickner, saying, "You know the way that you talk, you could jump off the Empire State Building and if it wasn't your time to die, nothing would happen to you. That's ridiculous." And Brickner answered, "No, no! I'm saying that I could be lying in my bed and the roof could fall on me, and if it was my time to go I would die that way." It turned into an argument, which amused our driver greatly, who just shook his head and said, "You'll find out, you'll find out."

Just two days later, on December 6th, 1944, we were back in our quarters at the base dressing for physical training. I had put on my shorts and shoes when mail call was announced. I sat down on a foot locker and began reading letters from home when suddenly we heard the sound of revving airplane engines overhead. The roaring got louder and louder and we realized the planes were coming towards us. I jumped up. Everyone was looking around wild-eyed, not sure what to do. Some guys were literally running in circles, while others ran out the back door. Then we heard a loud scraping sound on the peaked roof, and clouds of black ash and soot flew out of the stove, which moved around the floor. A terrible, bright orange flash lit up the room and the windows shattered. We thought it was the end of the world.

Two airplanes had collided over the barracks. One survived the collision and pulled away to limp back to the air field, but the other spun out of control. The engine raced as the pilot made a last-minute effort to pull out of the crash, but he went down, scraping the top of our quarters and crashing into the barracks right across the street, where my friend Brickner was in his upper bunk reading a letter from his girlfriend. A horrible smell of burned flesh hung in the air. Eleven men died, Brickner among them.

I was stricken by the amazing coincidence of this accident. I remembered my discussion with Brickner about fate and how he said he could be reading in bed and the roof could fall on him, and if it was his time to go, that would be the end of him. Brickner's death in that fateful crash was a very sobering experience for me. It wasn't my first experience with death, but it brought back to mind the words of my Grandmother Alcaria years before, when she admonished me to be ready to die at any time.

I graduated from the radio school and was sent to combat crew training at Alamogordo. There we went out on many practice missions. Each of us was assigned to a specific crew. I met and got to know my crew mates. The commanding officer was a stalwart Jewish fellow from Brooklyn, Irwin Stavin. The co-pilot Ted Marantette was a French Canadian from Maine; he had rosy cheeks and blond hair and was always jolly. The bombardier, Pascuarello was a very suave but sloppy Italian fellow from New Jersey. The navigator, Lacrosse, seemed shifty. The engineer Bob Waterhouse, from San Diego, California, who was a little older than the rest of us, presented a perfect physical specimen, with a flawless body—an Apollo figure. He was a champion swimmer and surf boarder. We called him "the Horse" because he seemed strong and perfect in every way. Then there were the gunners, Bob Simcox, Bruce Galbraith, Woody Teague and Bill Pearce; radar operator Belski, a Polish fellow from Chicago; and me, the radio operator—a gangly, young Hispanic from Santa Fe. We formed a close bond because we knew we were involved in dangerous business; fatal crashes were not uncommon.

After combat crew training they sent us to Topeka, Kansas, to be assigned a plane. We received a brand new B-29—a beautiful machine, and the most advanced bomber of its time. The air offensive against Japan was underway so we quickly organized, picked up our plane, and flew to Hawaii. After a brief stay there we continued across the Pacific to Kwajalein, where we saw sunken Japanese ships and evidence of battle, and then to Guam.

To our sorrow they took away our brand new plane on Guam and gave us an old one named Ready Betty that had already been in service and had flown several missions. We boarded our much-used plane and flew to our base on the island of Tinian. I was in the 58th bomb wing, the 48th bomb group and the 792nd squadron.

We lived in a Quonset hut made of bent metal. I planted papaya trees in front to spruce up the place, but there was little time for leisure. Almost at once we were sent on combat missions. I was the radio operator on the flight crew, but I also had other responsibilities. I sat next to the forward bomb bay, beside a round porthole-like window. Once on a mission, my first responsibility was to keep the radio open to instructions but silent so that the enemy couldn't locate us. In case of an emergency, of course, I could break the radio silence to let rescue personnel know where to find us.

The missions over Japan took on a terrifying sameness. As we approached our target we began to feel and see exploding anti-aircraft fire all around us, but we couldn't vary our course to avoid the flak because once we started on a designated bombing course and altitude we had to maintain it until we reached the designated bomb release point. When we reached the target the huge bomb bay doors would swing open and I would announce on the intercom, "Forward bomb bay is open." Then the bombardier would sight and press the button to drop the bombs. I would confirm that the bombs had been released, saying, "Bombs away!"

Several thousand feet below, I could plainly see the effects of our bombs. There were explosions everywhere, and masses of flames wherever we dropped incendiary bombs. Japanese houses are very combustible, and I saw entire cities in flames. Sometimes I'd say something bright like, "Those damn Japs are really getting it—we're killing thousands of them! It's great!? Revenge is wonderful!" Looking back now I'm appalled by my bloodthirsty attitude, but then I had no regrets whatsoever about what we were doing. I almost thought we were on a divine mission, doing what had to be done—which in the long run was probably true, because if there was ever a just war, World War II was it.

Once the bombs had fallen, I'd confirm the closing of the bomb bay doors and we'd head back to base. These missions lasted eleven to thirteen hours. They were exhausting, but we had to fly great distances to reach Japan from our nearest secure bases.

On one of my early missions we had to make an emergency landing on Iwo Jima, which the Marines had just captured. Taking the island exacted a great toll on our forces. The landing field had recently been graded, turning out human skeletons from foxholes and leaving bits of uniforms and bodies in plain sight. You can imagine what it smelled like. Iwo Jima was hell. Seeing the grisly aftermath of the battle there made me appreciate the terrible price that we had to pay to take enemy strongholds with ground forces. As the possibility of a land assault on Japan loomed, the sight reinforced my confidence that the air attacks were justified.

Going out on those long missions was a very maturing experience for me. I grew up quickly. Our missions took us to Okayama, Takamatsu, and to Sendai, which was a night mission and especially frightening. As we neared our target, Japanese searchlights went on, crisscrossing the sky looking for us. The B-29s weren't camouflaged; they were bright, silvery aluminum, so when the searchlights hit a plane, it showed up in a glint of brilliant silver. The beam of light would fix on the plane and track it, and soon other search lights would swing over to expose the bomber in a cone of brilliant light. Then the explosions of flak would begin.

On Friday the 13th of July 1945 we were on a bombing run to Utsunomiya, on Honshu. Just as we were getting close to our target, the sky became foggy and overcast. Belski said, "My radar has gone out. With all this fog, we're not going to be able to make the bomb run. I'm not sure we'd be hitting the target." We always had a secondary target, and on this particular day it was Chosi Point—a peninsula jutting into Tokyo Bay where the Japanese had oil tank farms. It was very heavily defended, so news that we had to attack Chosi cast a pall over the crew.

We changed course and dropped our bombs on Chosi Point, but the clouds were so thick that I couldn't tell if we hit the tank farm or if the bombs landed in the Bay of Tokyo. We were besieged by heavy anti-aircraft fire and when we started back for our base it was evident that we had been hit. One of our four engines failed. The pilot feathered its propeller—then the other engine on the same side started causing problems. The commander said, "We may not make it to Iwo Jima. Frank, get on your radio and let them know we're in distress and that we may have to go down in the ocean. See if they can help us because I don't think we can make Iwo."

Remembering that day brings it all back so vividly. I recall the pilot saying, "We're going down! Dump anything heavy that is loose." So I opened the round door/hatch into the bomb bay and the crew passed everything heavy that could fly about and we threw it all into the bomb bay. I locked the hatch, securing the loose gear within. At this point we were losing altitude and it was obvious we were going to go down. Fortunately, Stavin was a very good pilot. His idea was to put the plane down in the valley between two big waves, to lessen the impact. He feathered the propellers on the functioning engines so that they were not spinning and we glided down toward the water. It was a good plan, but there was a problem: the plane's wingspread was so great that, as we hit the water, the left wing caught in a wave, which spun the plane around. Instead of gliding into the valley between waves, we crashed headlong into one.

The impact delivered an incredible shock. The aluminum of the fuselage screamed as it was torn and ripped apart. Then of a sudden, after the catastrophic noise, there was absolute silence—for just a moment. And then the water started rushing in and I heard the groans of distress around me.

Without thinking, I began to do my job—not because I was a hero or especially smart, but because we'd been drilled in the emergency routines so often that I couldn't think of anything else to do. I stood up and pulled releases for two small, self-inflating rubber life rafts. Then I opened the hatch of the astrodome—a clear plastic dome where the navigator sat to make observations of the stars. It became clear to me that the plane was broken in half just behind the wings, its nose filling with water. I climbed out of the plane and into a raft and tried to help others to join me. The plane was pointed downward, nose-first, and began to sink rapidly. The tail broke off and was also going under. As we bobbed there on the raft, the huge, rolling swells on the ocean terrified me. The Pacific is a very scary place when you're on a life raft; you're nothing in the middle of nowhere. We were about half-way between Japan and Iwo Jima—very, very far from land.

The guys in the back of the plane also got into a little raft, except for Bill Pearce, who wouldn't turn loose of the tail. As the tail sank he went down with it. We heard him screaming. Bill Teague swam off, away from the plane and the raft. He was afraid of being sucked under by the sinking plane when he saw what had happened to Pearce. But he apparently was badly hurt and bleeding because very shortly shark fins appeared and we heard him screaming. That was the last time we saw him alive.

I was in the front of the raft, scanning the water for the two pilots and the crew from the front of the plane, who were still under water. They finally surfaced and I helped them into the rafts. During all this commotion, our "hero," Bob Waterhouse, the great Olympic swimmer, swam away effortlessly. While the plane was sinking and crewmates were dying and others were struggling onto the rafts, he paddled far away and watched. He waited until the plane had sunk and then, when the chaos was over and we'd done everything we could to save ourselves, he smoothly swam back and climbed aboard the raft.

I had screwed the key on my radio set down, which sent out a signal to help the rescue people locate us. Soon a PBY plane dropped a larger life raft for us and we climbed out of the little ones and into the big one. Not long afterwards a patrol craft picked us up and took us to Iwo Jima. Teague's mauled body was recovered, and he was buried on Iwo.

None of us talked to Waterhouse after the crash. As an excuse for his cowardly behavior, he lamely said he had a family to consider and we did not. Unconvinced, we turned our backs on him and wanted nothing to do with him. He had abandoned us in time of crisis, shattering his image in our minds of a strong and reliable crewmate.

That crash brought me closer to death than I'd ever been before. I remember that as we were going down, all I could think to say as I braced for the impact was "Thy will be done, thy kingdom come." I also remember that I was wearing a baseball cap with a big bill and high, laced up boots. Oddly, when I was picked up the baseball cap was still on my head but my boots had been blown off. Afterwards, I found that I had a small wound on one leg but was otherwise physically intact.

After the crash, the crew was finished. We had lost two crewmates and some survivors were terribly traumatized. I was assigned to another crew and went back on combat missions. I guess they immediately sent men back into action because, as the adage says, if you fall off a horse, you have to get right back on it. But I felt terrible as I went back into action. I was reliving the awful experience in my mind every day.

Fortunately, the war ended shortly after the plane crash, when the atomic bombs were dropped on Hiroshima and Nagasaki. The planes that carried the atomic bombs were based with my Wing on Tinian. We had no knowledge of this and were perplexed when we were issued pistols and rifles and were drilled in how to repel invasions. I realized later that we were being trained to respond in the event that the Japanese attacked to destroy the bombers and their nuclear payload.

For a while after Japan's surrender, I continued to fly relief missions, dipping low over prisoner of war camps in Japan to drop food and medicines. The prisoners would write "POW" in giant letters on their rooftops and we'd drop them food, cigarettes, chocolate bars, and Cokes. Often I was worried we'd kill our own men by dropping heavy packages on them.

On September 2, 1945, when Japan's surrender was signed on the deck of the USS Missouri, there was a great parade, with hundreds of huge bombers flying low over Tokyo Bay. Aboard one of the planes, I looked down and saw figures on the deck of the Missouri as they signed the surrender. Tokyo was in ruins.

While flying a support mission on September 20th 1945, I collapsed and started coughing up blood. I was carried off to the hospital, where X-rays revealed that I had tuberculosis in my upper right lung. I had been losing weight and was thin as a stick, no meat on me at all. I was medically evacuated to the United States on a hospital plane. The guy on the pallet next to me had been shot up terribly and was in excruciating pain. Medics were giving him shots of morphine constantly. I felt that my world had come to an end but, after seeing him and some others—many amputees and burn victims—I felt I was lucky. I had survived more or less intact. And I had come to a greater appreciation for the whims of fate.

As I puzzled about how I had contracted the tuberculosis, I remembered that a cousin in Santa Fe had a diary when I was growing up. Until we acquired our own dairy cow, we bought milk from Leopoldo—and I doubt that he pasteurized it. When I mentioned this to the doctor, he told me that the TB had probably been latent in my system for years. He sent me to Fitzsimmons Hospital, in Aurora, Colorado, on the outskirts of Denver, for treatment. In those days, the treatment for TB involved inserting a huge, hollow needle between the ribs and pumping air into the chest cavity, which collapsed the lung against the spinal column. Once it was immobilized, the lung could heal more effectively.

The treatments went on for about three years, initially on a weekly basis, then, in the second year, monthly and finally, in the third year, every three months. It was excruciatingly painful at times, especially when the needle missed and hit a rib. I developed a high level of pain tolerance as well as great patience: I had to lie flat on my back for a year. But I learned a lot from the experience, especially from seeing so many others in rehabilitation, a lot of them much worse off than I.

I had been away from Santa Fe just over two years, but felt I had been away ages. My experiences in Washington, in active combat, and during rehabilitation had turned my world upside down. Taken altogether, these experiences taught me lessons that convinced me to redirect my life.

The combat crew of the B-29 Bomber "Ready Betty," 1945

Under attack over Japan. From *The 20th Air Force Album* by Richard M. Keenan, published by the 20th Air Force Association

Being rescued by a naval patrol craft Friday, July 13, 1945
(*Brief* magazine, August 28, 1945)

Georgetown University School of Foreign Service, 1948

3

Into America's Front Line Trenches: Passing the Exams and a Special Mission to the Sudan

A medical discharge from the Air Force allowed me to come home to continue my TB treatment regime. I went out to the ranch to recuperate between treatments. Since I was immobilized, I used the time to read *War and Peace, The Remembrance of Things Past, Don Quixote, The Education of Henry Adams,* and many other great books that I had always wanted to read. I read and read and my condition improved steadily.

During this time I also did some deep soul searching. My hope had been to be a doctor in Santa Fe, but the experiences of combat duty, the plane crash, and my prolonged and painful illness prompted me to take a different tack. I also was moved in no small measure by the loss of so many friends in the war and by regrets about my role in destroying cities and killing people. I concluded that I had to do something to make the world better. My first impulse was to be a missionary priest—a thought that brought with it a ghostly pat on the back from Grandmother Alcaria. But I was twenty years old with strong hormonal surges and I knew I wanted a family. It didn't take me too long to decide against being a priest, but I had to think of something else to do to "save the world."

About that time I read a book about a diplomat who, through his service, helped resolve conflicts peacefully—an approach that seemed more sensible than warfare. That inspired me toward the foreign service and in 1947—about two years after my catastrophe—I applied to the Georgetown University School of Foreign Service.

My acceptance at Georgetown confirmed for me that my education in the Santa Fe Public Schools had been excellent. Georgetown was a wonderful school with the finest Foreign Service program in the country. Resolving to go there was one of the best decisions I ever made. The school challenged me rigorously. There, as in Santa Fe, I was fortunate to have extraordinary teachers who had a significant impact on me. From my great professors Carroll Quigley and Jules David I learned that a good education is being made aware of what you don't know.

I was doing very well at the university when I decided to take the Foreign Service exam to become a U.S. diplomat. It's a very tough exam. I signed up for it in my junior year, thinking that I would take it again seriously the next year. I had learned from my experience in the flight simulator during basic training for the Air Force to give things a trial run first, before the real test.

I was so relaxed while taking that test that I whizzed through it. When I didn't know the answer to a question, I just moved on to the next. I didn't sweat over it. If I wasn't sure of the answer, I would risk a guess. The test lasted three days. I zipped through the multiple-choice questions and took my time with the essays. I chose Spanish for my foreign language. To my amazement I passed the exam—not brilliantly but I passed it. I also passed oral exams before an intimidating panel of senior Ambassadors.

The State Department invited me to enter the Service right away, skipping my senior year at Georgetown. I could have done that, but my college degree was more important to me—a priority I learned from my parents and also imparted to my children. When I did earn my degree from Georgetown, I again could have begun working with the Service immediately. But I had a strong urge to travel, especially to Europe. I saw that the time was ripe, before committing myself to a career. My friend and classmate Bill Leonard was of the same mind, so we planned a European tour. Just the prospect of a summer in Europe filled me with unbridled joy.

My first stop was Spain, where I studied Spanish—the King's Spanish—while Bill was in England. The Spanish experience turned out to be very worthwhile, with much of the payoff to come years later, when I worked on Spanish affairs for the Department of State. From Spain, I joined Bill in Paris, where we had arranged to share a fine apartment for a month in the best part of the city. We also had reserved an automobile to tour France, Switzerland, Germany, Austria, Italy, Spain, and Morocco.

That European tour exceeded all my expectations and sharpened my appetite for foreign travel. All along the way, thanks to many friends, we enjoyed the best of the countries we visited. I was especially smitten with Italy and Spain and resolved to return, which I did often over the next 50 years.

A problem did develop during that Europe tour, however—one that caused me much consternation but taught me a very valuable lesson. While I was in Spain, Bill fell head-over-heels in love with a sophisticated, elegant French woman. It seemed to me, a protective pal, that Bill was diving into water way over his head. I believed Bill was too young and naïve to become seriously involved with a foreign woman of such obviously sophisticated origins. I considered it my responsibility to save Bill from the clutches of someone I feared was a European femme fatal. Of course I never asked Bill, who was deeply in love, if he needed saving.

As we traveled throughout Europe, I did everything I could to dissuade Bill from staying involved with the French woman. Even when I returned to the States (while Bill stayed in France), I did what I could to break up his infatuation with his charming lady, but my efforts were in vain. I soon received an invitation for Bill's wedding in Paris.

I was dismayed, but needn't have been. Their relationship worked out beautifully, and their marriage has lasted for decades. I was dead wrong to have interfered, but, fortunately, they both forgave me—and the experience taught me how profound the power of love can be. As the tango lyric says, "Love has such great power that it carries all before it." Up until that experience with Bill and his sweetheart, I had not believed in mad, passionate love. I was glad that such a powerful lesson came early in my life.

When I returned to the U.S., the State Department wanted me to start work immediately, but I faced one last obstacle to entering the Foreign Service: I had to pass a review by the Medical Board, which was headed by a tough old doctor named DeVault. When I went before the board, DeVault said, "How did you get here?" I said, "What do you mean, how did I get here? I passed the exams." "But," DeWalt said, "you received a medical discharge from the Army Air Force. You've had tuberculosis, so there is no way you can serve in the American Foreign Service. There is no way we could send you anywhere, especially anyplace at a high elevation. We're sorry but we don't know how you got this far. We reject you."

I learned how to handle profound disappointment that day, but soon after that blow, the personnel division at the State Department wrote to me. They apologized for mistreating a disabled veteran, but they still couldn't accept me into the Foreign Service. Instead, they assigned me to the Near East Office at the State Department, as a deputy to a great professional, Wells Stabler. In other words, I had a great job at the State Department, but I was condemned to the home office—a prospect that didn't exactly fulfill my dreams.

I was about 26 when I landed that first job with the State Department, and it was during my tenure there that I met my wife Dolores. The timing was right. Since I had a good job, I had made up my mind it was time to get married. I have always been the kind of person who acts deliberately; when I make up my mind to do something, I do it. So I consciously started out to look for a good candidate to be my wife, and there were certain attributes that I felt she had to have, including good looks. I took every opportunity to meet attractive girls.

I dated an exquisitely beautiful woman, Maria Teresa. Her beauty was such that once when we double-dated with Jackie Kennedy, who was still Jacqueline Bouvier, Maria Teresa put Jackie in the shade. Jackie seemed fey and self-conscious. She spoke in a whisper, and kept every hair in place and every detail of her clothing perfect. She carried herself carefully, with an aristocratic air, and you'd have to lean forward to hear what she was saying. I didn't find her very exciting. But my date, Maria Teresa—the daughter of an Ambassador—had many of the qualities I sought. But unfortunately, in spite of her beauty, I felt no physical attraction toward her.

I also dated the remarkable daughter of the Air Attaché of the Spanish Embassy, while I was still in college. Marina was a fine person, and very beautiful. She had flashing eyes and much verve. I was very taken with her. She later became a good friend to Dolores and we often visited her in Spain, but at the time her parents were very domineering and didn't like the fact that Marina would have to stay in America if she married me. So our relationship was a dead end and Marina eventually went back to Spain.

I remained actively on the hunt. I began seeing a girl named Missy. My guardian angel saved me from getting seriously involved with her, but meeting her did lead me to the right person. One day Missy's mother called to tell me she was planning a reception and inviting important people from the State Department. "Since you will marry my daughter and work in the State Department, I want you to know these people," she said. She warned me that Missy, her sister, and I would be the only young people there, so it would be a boring evening. But, she assured me, I would meet people who could be important for my career.

I accepted the invitation and went to the party. Missy was very difficult that night. Some little thing upset her, and she stomped off to her bedroom to sulk. That left me alone with people who were very much my seniors—army officers, Ambassadors, and officials of the State Department. As I mingled awkwardly among them, I looked across the room, and there was a girl that really did something for me. That was Dolores.

Dolores was at the party with her parents. Her mother, Guadalupe, was from Durango, Mexico. She was the most beautiful of U.S. Army wives, and famous for it. When I spotted these stunning women—Dolores, and her mother—and learned that they spoke Spanish, I zipped right across the room to meet them. I fell in love with Dolores right that second and decided then and there that I was going to marry her. (We both now believe in divine intervention.)

At that first meeting, I spontaneously invited Dolores to see a play, *The Dark of the Moon.* At that time, I lived with the Juraj Slavik family. Slavik was the last democratic Czech Ambassador to the U.S. When the communists took over in Czechoslovakia, he resigned and stayed in Washington. He owned a big house and took in boarders. That very night I announced to Mama and Papa Slavik that I'd met the woman I was going to marry. That's how sure I was that she was the one for me. She was beautiful. She was Catholic. And she had Spanish ancestry. She had everything that I wanted. But, I wondered, did she feel the same way about me?

Dolores' father, Brigadier General James Thomas Duke, was the commanding officer of Fort Myer, which overlooks Washington. The ranking military officers—the chiefs of staff and other high-ups—lived there. Dolores didn't live in one of the great mansions, but in one of the row houses at the fort. She had just come back from Europe, where she'd lived for five years.

Dolores already knew something of the world. Her enthusiasm for me seemed under control, but she knew I cared for her. She had been engaged to a Frenchman, and when that broke up, there was an Englishman and then a Colombian. The Colombian was very good looking, but thanks to my lucky stars he was sent off to Korea. With him gone, she more or less had to pay attention to me. I could tell she began to like me. Having considered the choice of being *Madame* Ganival, Mrs. Snellgrove, or *Señora* Hanaberger, she now thought about becoming Mrs. Ortiz.

Meeting Dolores was the highlight of my eventful personal life during my early tenure at the State Department. I was also doing quite well in my professional life. I took well to Arabs and Arabic at the Near East office, perhaps because I'm a northern New Mexican. As with all Hispanic communities, there's a strong Moorish influence in our culture.

In 1951, the year I met Dolores and only a few months into my service as the junior officer on the Egyptian/Anglo Egyptian/Sudan Desk, I was sent to Egypt. There, through my friendship with Bill Lakeland, a brilliant young officer in Embassy Cairo, I met many highly-placed Egyptians, including some of King Farouk's court, members of the main Egyptian political parties, and newspaper owners. The most interesting person I got to know was a young army officer named Gamal Abdel Nasser. He loved to eat turkey, so Bill invited him over for a turkey meal twice while I was in Cairo. Nasser was on the staff of a senior army officer, General Naguib, who with other officers was planning to overthrow King Farouk. We didn't know that then, but it explains the officers' friendliness with our embassy; they were courting contacts in anticipation of taking power.

At a swish party after my return to Washington, I heard myself bragging about my great success at meeting important Egyptians and how they seemed to take to me. A woman earnestly confronted me, saying that I clearly would not succeed in the Foreign Service if I sought out only the rich and powerful. "What I want to know," she said, "is what common Egyptians—the masses—think about the U.S. and its policies." She asked if I had traveled into the slums of the cities and the countryside to talk to the common folk. I realized that I had been so swept up in Cairo's elite centers that I hadn't spoken with many ordinary people. That woman's comments took the wind out of my sails. I imagined that those present saw me as a neophyte with not much future. I left the party early feeling crushed.

On my next visit to Egypt, King Farouk was out, General Naguib was in power, and Colonel Nasser was preparing to push Naguib aside. I renewed my relationships in Cairo, except for the out-of-power Farouk courtiers. Nasser had gained weight and along with the weight had taken on an aura of power. He kept his distance from me, acting aloof. Responding to the woman's comments in Washington, I insisted a young Egyptian friend take me into the slums and into the countryside and interpret for me to learn what the "Egyptian people" really thought.

The experience was sobering. Of the dozens of common men and women with whom I spoke, only one or two knew that America was a country far away and not a village up the Nile—if they had any idea about the U.S. at all. In short, their views and opinions were of little help to me in my responsibilities regarding Egypt. When I mentioned this to a powerful newsman, Mohammed Heikal, he smiled and said that it was he, his colleagues, the elite, and the government that decided what the common man thought about the U.S. and its policies. He recommended I concentrate on the power elite and not worry about the common folk.

While Heikal was right in a cynical way, over the span of my career I found that in high political spheres often there was not much common sense—or what we call horse sense in the West. Ordinary folk, on the other hand, have a surfeit of common sense, and ignoring their opinions can be a grave mistake. Although not ruled by it, I tried always to gauge public opinion. It is a fact that in the long run—and often even in the short term—the wishes of general populace can be the deciding factor.

A year and a half after those previous visits to Egypt, Dolores and I stopped in Cairo as newlyweds on our way to Ethiopia. Heikal invited us for an elaborate dinner. My main course—different than what was presented to the others—was a large platter of goat testicles. I never figured out if Heikal was indulging in an Egyptian tradition relating to new bridegrooms or if he was signaling that I needed to stop being an idealistic chump and toughen up.

During my assignment to the State Department's Egyptian desk, my easy acceptance of and by Arabs prompted the department to train me to become a Middle East expert. They sent me to the American University of Beirut, Lebanon, to study the area and the language.

I left Washington for Beirut in 1952, embarking on an incredible experience. While there, I was able to make trips to Israel and other countries of the Middle East. I came in contact with this ancient part of the world, where our civilization began. I was as happy as could be. I visited ruins and reveled in old cities like Damascus, Istanbul and of course Jerusalem, which back then was still part of Jordan.

In Jerusalem, I stayed in a Polish nuns' convent, Dom Polski. At night the gates to Old Jerusalem closed and the whole city was enclosed in the walls. I woke at two in the morning one night. I dressed and went out to walk through the city, lit by a full moon. The streets were empty, and the only noise came from a few barking dogs. I walked along the walls of the city, down the Via Dolorosa, and along crooked, narrow little streets. I was inspired to write a letter to Dolores that night, proposing marriage. She accepted. I had found celestially inspired, true, passionate love. A brass crucifix I bought in Jerusalem graces the headboard of our matrimonial bed—and has remained with us for fifty years.

The culmination of my stay in the Middle East came when I was chosen, along with Bill Lakeland, to fly to Khartoum in the Sudan. Bill (who spoke perfect Arabic) and I took the naval attaché's plane from Cairo to Khartoum. Our assignment was to make a report to our government as to whether the Sudanese would opt for independence or if they would want to remain under the co-dominion of the British and the Egyptians.

We flew low over the magical Nile River all the way up to Khartoum, past marvelous historic sites: Luxor, the Valley of the Kings, Meroe. The Sudanese received us royally in Khartoum. Sayed Rahman al Mahdi, the posthumous son of the Mahdi, was an imposing leader of the faction against British rule. Sayed al Mirgani, who was lying in a little bed, also told us the country was going to go for independence. "Don't believe anything anyone else tells you," he said. "It's going to come."

Bill and I reported to our government that independence was certain. We turned out to be right, which was good for our reputations. (Unfortunately Bill, who was a premier Arabist, left the Service after an unsuccessful career, as did many of his Arabist specialists.)

When I came back from my studies in the Middle East I was a minor Arabist. I had done well enough to convince the Board of the Foreign Service, the ultimate authority in these matters, that I would do well overseas. They overruled Dr. DeValt and the medical department and brought me in as an officer of the Service. Just like that I was in the Foreign Service at last, and a dream that had once seemed shattered became whole.

Once we knew that my future was assured, Dolores and I were married, in May of 1953, at the Ft. Meyer Chapel. That led to more than fifty years of partnership. Dolores became a key element in my success in the Foreign Service.

My first assignment in the Service came immediately, to Damascus, Syria, which meant that we had only two days of honeymoon before we began preparations to leave. On our way to eastern Maryland for our honeymoon, we stopped for a milkshake. I put a nickel in a slot machine and won the jackpot. We took it as a good omen. We were off to a great start.

4

Reassignment Ethiopia: At the Emperor's Court and Following in Burton's Footsteps

When we learned of our assignment to Damascus, Dolores and I began intensive courses in Damascene Arabic. When our course was done, the Syrian Embassy gave us a farewell party sending us off to Syria. But just at that time there was a reduction in force, and the job in Damascus disappeared. We were assigned instead to Ethiopia—where Arabic is not a common language.

We were stunned. All my career plans again seemed to be falling apart, but it turned out to be a very positive change. We set sail on the American Export Line out of New York. I ran like a madman to Macys's to buy a top hat to go with my hand-me-down morning coat to be properly attired for the Ethiopian court, which was extremely protocol conscious.

We barely made the boat on time and sailed across the Atlantic to Italy. We disembarked at Naples and traveled to Rome to visit our friends, Wells Stabler and his beautiful new wife Emily. I convinced Dolores, who was four months pregnant, to climb to the top of St. Peter's dome—against her better judgment. We visited other sites in Rome and then boarded a plane to Ethiopia, with a stop in Cairo. When we finally landed in Addis Ababa, Dolores seemed about to have a miscarriage and had to take to her bed. She held on to full term and gave birth to lovely Tina, our first child.

In Addis Ababa, I assumed my position as Third Secretary of the embassy—the lowest officer rank in the Service. In addition to being the Third Secretary I was head of the consular service for Somalia and British and French Somaliland. A vast territory full of wild places comprised my parish. We were assigned quarters that had previously been horse stables. The low building, situated inside the high walls of the Embassy compound, had wide double Dutch doors and had a beautiful garden because of the deep layers of accumulated manure. Our associates at the Embassy pitied us, saying, "You poor things! They really gave you the pits." Most of the compound houses were brand new with all the modern conveniences, and we landed in a so-called dump. But Dolores turned it into one of the most beautiful houses in East Africa. Its large, long, high-ceilinged rooms proved perfect for entertaining large groups, which we did to great success.

Back then, East Africa was like a scene out of the Arabian Nights. Harar in Ethiopia was wonderful, and Kenya was still untrammeled—but unstable, I might add. I happened to be in Nairobi, on my way back to Ethiopia from Aden, during the Mau Mau rebellion. The rebels murdered members of the Leaky family that week.

Addis Ababa was a very small, tranquil community without much going on. There was only one restaurant, which served terrible food, and one movie theater. It seemed the entire country was flea-ridden. When we'd go to see movies, for example, we had to take along bug spray to fend off the countless fleas in the theater seats—but when we returned to our home we still had to undress in the bathtub to contain and flush the fleas jumping off us.

Ethiopia was under the reign of Haile Selassie, His Imperial Majesty, the King of Kings, Conquering Lion of Judah, Emperor of Ethiopia. The three imperial princes of Ethiopia, all sons of the Emperor, were the Crown Prince, the Duke of Harar, and Prince Sahle Selassie. I especially liked Sahle, a talented, almost effeminate person with very frizzy hair. Most Ethiopians have curly hair, but his was frizzier than most. One day, resolved to straighten those wild curls, he sent off for a chemical pomade. Unfortunately, the treatment caused him permanently to lose great patches of hair. He became reclusive after that.

By chance I learned that Sahle loved *Gourmet* magazine. He had come across a copy somewhere and couldn't get over the wonderful things he saw in it. Friends in the states sent me a stack of the magazines and I presented them to the Prince, which delighted him greatly. We found that little gestures like this helped us establish relationships with Ethiopians, who are very reserved people. They consider it improper to touch physically, for example. Theirs is a very old, rich and formal culture.

We enjoyed great success in Addis. Ethiopians came to our parties and gatherings in droves. We had created all our own entertainment and came up with some novel activities. I often brought out the bathroom scales and passed them around to the men, who would compete to see who could press the scale with his hands to the highest number. Meanwhile, Dolores presented Sears Roebuck catalogs to the beautiful Ethiopian women, who crowded on the couch to flip with fascination through their pages. On our lawn I set up a croquet set, adding speed bumps and sand traps for extra challenge and diversion. Dolores made a roulette set out of pieces of old, green cloth and a buggy wheel.

Word got around about how much fun we were having and in no time members of the nobility, other powerful people, and even members of the imperial family became friends. Endalkatchew Makonnen, whose father was Prime Minister, came often. Dolores did extraordinary things to cement our relationships with these people.

One time Endalkatchew brought a lovely girl named Encanyelish to meet us because, he announced, he was going to marry her. She was all of fourteen years old. After presenting her, Endalkatchew took her back to her house and returned to ask our opinion of her. We told him we liked her a lot, but Dolores added, "You know, she is very young, and she hasn't finished school yet." Endalkatchew thought that wasn't important. Dolores advised him that Encanyelish would someday be the mother of his children and asked, "Don't you want your children to have an educated mother, one suited to accompany you? Because you're surely going to be Prime Minister." "Well," Endalkatchew replied, "She's so beautiful that somebody else will get her if I don't marry her now." Dolores offered to find a school in England for Encanyelish, where she would be safe from would-be Ethiopian suitors. Endalkatchew agreed and Encanyelish enrolled in an English girls school.

We left Ethiopia before Encanyelish returned from her schooling, but many years later in New York Endalkatchew served as Ethiopia's Ambassador to the United Nations. When we called on him there, he couldn't thank us enough for encouraging Encanyelish to get an education. Unfortunately, we didn't see Encanyelish because she was away, but apparently she had turned out to be not only a fine mother, but also an intelligent community leader. Sadly Encanyelish, Endalkatchew, and many other dear friends were murdered when the Marxists took over in Ethiopia in 1974.

One day a call came for me at the Embassy. The receptionist who ran the switch board was almost shaking with nervousness when she said, "The Lord Chamberlain wants to talk to you." The Chamberlain, Ato Tafara Worq, called to say that His Imperial Majesty had heard of the good times young Ethiopians were having at our home. He told me that Emperor "commanded" me to appear at the Filwoha Hotel Ballroom (the best hotel in town) the next Sunday afternoon. "The Imperial children will be there," Ato Tafara added, " and you must give them lessons in the amusing parlor games that you play. His Imperial Majesty wants them to learn these games to enliven the affairs at the palace."

Given a directive like that, of course I couldn't say no. We brushed up on parlor games described in a game book and went to the hotel that Sunday. A group of angelic kids five to twelve years of age showed up, dressed in their best clothes and accompanied by nannies. "Okay, children," I announced, "we're going to play musical chairs." We lined up the chairs and showed them how the game worked. They caught on quickly, marching around and then scrambling for seats when we paused the music. They loved it, but the trouble was that they cheated, four or five of them at a time crowding into a chair. We couldn't convince them to play by the rules, so that game didn't work so well.

Then we tried Pin-the-Tail-on-the-Donkey, and they loved it, too—but they all preferred to pull the blindfold down and peek. We taught them Spin the Bottle, and again they found ways to get around the rules. And so it went. The games didn't work out as we knew them, but the children had a great time anyway.

It was through these unusual little actions—giving the prince Gourmet magazine, playing parlor games with the kids—that we were able to become close to important decision-makers in Ethiopia. That helped us accomplish our mission.

Our official goal in Ethiopia was to foment economic development, especially in agriculture. A large group from Oklahoma A&M worked wonders in this regard. Thanks to the Oklahomans' work, the world learned that coffee originated in Ethiopia's Kaffa region, which now exports premium brands. We also strove to nudge the government to adopt a constitutional monarchy on the road to democracy. The Empire was very autocratic, with no control on the power of the Emperor, Haile Selassie. A couple of American lawyers came to help draft a new constitution. I had a minor role in that, but it turned out to be a disaster for the Emperor. In 1974, long after we left Ethiopia, he loosened control, and a rebellion supported by the Soviets put Marxists in power. The Marxists murdered Selassie along with many of our friends. Ethiopia then entered a disastrous period of decline from which it still has not recovered.

My assignments were many and varied during my tenure in Ethiopia. The American Ambassador for whom I worked had no foreign service experience at all and didn't entirely understand what was involved in running an embassy. He assumed that since I had spent two years in the State Department, I was an expert. That assumption wasn't at all accurate! I had a lot to learn. It was often the little details that vexed me. Once at an important embassy party, for example, he put me in charge of the bar, not realizing that I had no experience mixing drinks. I was to oversee the mixing of martinis, but used sweet vermouth instead of dry vermouth. Everybody complained.

After two years in Ethiopia, I faced a much larger task—one that involved a thorough understanding of Ethiopian court protocol. The Emperor planned a huge celebration of the 25th anniversary of his accession to the throne. President Eisenhower sent a distinguished group of Americans to represent the United States at the balls, banquets, military displays, and ceremonies that would mark this great event. The Ambassador informed me that, as the protocol officer, I would have to drill the American delegation in matters of Ethiopian court etiquette, which was strict and modeled after the Swedish court.

I assembled the American delegation their first night in town to instruct them on protocol. The delegation included a military man and several others. I especially remember two of the members: Mrs. Robert Low Bacon, who presided over a mansion in Washington one block from the White House and who was the doyenne of Washington society; and a tall, aristocratic man from Boston named Sears, who announced right off, "I'm of the Sears family of Boston." For most of us, that meant zero.

I explained to the delegation the plans for a main event of the celebration, the formal ceremony of presentation to the Emperor, cautioning them that the formalities could be intimidating. I described how the delegations from the various countries would be presented to the Emperor as he sat on his throne in a grand hall with the Ethiopian court lined up on both sides of the room. The delegations were to enter through large doors at the end of the room, where the Chamberlain, staff in hand, would formally present each group to the Emperor. When our turn came, the Chamberlain would loudly announce, "Delegation of the President of the United States." That would be our cue to enter the hall and bow or curtsy, according to gender—an act we had to repeat two more times as we walked slowly toward the Emperor's throne, once halfway up the aisle and again as we stood before the Emperor.

I made it clear that it would be considered improper to hold out a hand toward the Emperor or to talk to him, unless he reached out or spoke first. We were to be among the last delegations to enter, with all the other delegations and the court watching, so we had to be especially careful to conduct ourselves according to protocol. Since we could not turn our backs to the Emperor and the Empress, the trickiest maneuver was to back away from them gracefully.

In the midst of my presentation, Sears stood up and said, "Do my ears deceive me? Is it possible that an American official is telling Americans that they have to bow before a foreign ruler? I'm a Sears of Boston and will not do that. I am shocked that you would even suggest it. Is this your idea young man?" I assured him that it was not my idea but that the Ambassador wanted me to teach everyone what was correct by Ethiopian standards. Sears sniffed and told me to tell the Ambassador that he would not do it, then he left for his hotel.

The delegation knew Sears and told me not to pay attention to him, but I realized his refusal to bow would insult the Emperor and create a scandal. I reported this to the Ambassador, who recognized the seriousness of the problem but passed off the task of finding a solution to me. The Ambassador was so nervous and upset that he was no help at all. "Frank, I know you'll think of something," he said.

I went home and thought about it and came up with an idea. I immediately called on Sears at his hotel. It was late and Sears had retired to his room, but I rang from downstairs and told him that I must see him. He grumpily agreed to talk with me, but was quite rude when I knocked at the door.

"I'm concerned," I told Sears. "You have such a fine reputation—you're number two to Senator Warren, the head of the American delegation to the United Nations. You're very well known, and you've had a brilliant career. It will certainly tarnish your reputation when it becomes public knowledge that you refuse to bow to Emperor Haile Selassie because he's black." That got his attention. He stood up and said, "That's not it at all. I'm not going to bow because I believe that Americans shouldn't bow to anybody." I assured him that I understood but pointed out it wouldn't look that way to others. "Do you really believe people are going to think I'm racist?" he asked. "Sir, how else are they going to take it?" I replied. He thought a minute and then agreed. He asked me to tell him again how he should behave during the ceremony, and I drilled him right there in his hotel room.

The day of the ceremony, the men of the delegation wearing morning coats and top hats, the ladies in fine gowns, we took our places in line at the palace. When the Chamberlain announced the Delegation of the President of the United States, we entered into a room filled with people. Just as scripted, the court and the foreign delegations were lined up along the sides of the room, while His Imperial Majesty and the Empress sat on their thrones at the head of the room. The men bowed and the women curtsied. Sears' nose almost touched the floor. We reached the center of the room, and he bowed deeply again while his escort, Mrs. Low Bacon, curtsied. Finally we stood before the throne. I was behind everybody and I could see that Sears was very nervous. He became a little confused and glanced at Ms. Lowe, and lo and behold, he curtsied when she did. You could hear the titters all up and down the room. It was a deliciously funny moment. I hope word of it never reached Boston.

When my wife Dolores was presented to the Empress, she began to curtsy, but as she was about seven months pregnant, the whole back of her dress ripped out. Fortunately one of the ladies had a *rebozo* and quickly covered her, so Dolores recovered and carried off her presentation beautifully.

That was but one small event in many that kept us busy and happy in Ethiopia. We also had many extraordinary experiences outside of our diplomatic responsibilities. One of these was an expedition to Lalibela, in the province of Shoa. There Christians carved out of stone twelve extraordinary, underground churches in the twelfth century. Ethiopia was Christian before Europe and remains devoutly so. When the Muslims invaded the kingdom, the Christians fled to very high, cold, isolated places to hide. There they carved, extraordinary, underground churches out of living rock. I was among the first Americans to visit Lalibela.

It took our expedition of six westerners eight days on mules to make the trip to Lalibela. We carried a letter from our friend the Crown Prince that authorized our visit to some of Lalibela's secret places. We delivered the letter to the High Priest of Lalibela, who accompanied us during our visit. We brought with us big, powerful flashlights and went underground in the dark to admire the churches. The straw on the floor was crawling with fleas—thousands of them—but the underground churches were an awesome sight.

I knew that the reputation I established in Ethiopia would be important for my future in the Foreign Service. Fortunately, my tenure there successfully launched my professional career. Perhaps my most widespread recognition came in an unsuspected way, however, with my involvement in a rather nutty event. It was my introduction to peers in the Foreign Service throughout the world.

The Crown Prince of Ethiopia had married his daughter off to the family of powerful nobles. This greatly strengthened the royal family and was a coup for them, so the prince planned a magnificent party for the marriage feast. Inside a big tent, dozens of tables were set with fine porcelains, silver, and crystal from Europe. A great show was planned to entertain the guests at the festivities.

As preparations for the feast were underway, Dolores and I happened to be at the airport, which was one of the main sources of entertainment in Addis Ababa. Lacking other diversions, we would often go to the airport to see who was leaving or arriving.

We were observing the airport scene when suddenly, at the top of the arriving plane's staircase, there appeared an incredible creature: a peroxide blonde, to all appearances your classic bimbo, sporting a feather boa, very high heels and a very short skirt. Nobody in Ethiopia had ever seen anything like that. As she flounced off the plane, Dolores said, "I'll bet she's German." And I said, "No. No European woman would do that. I'll bet she's American." We joked about this woman's outrageous appearance all the way back home.

I hadn't thought much about the incident the next morning when I was at my office in the embassy and the receptionist came in and announced, "There's an incredible woman here who wants to see the consular officer." Much to my astonishment, in came the creature we had seen at the airport. She wouldn't sit in the chair I offered but instead sat on the edge of my desk and leaned over me, plainly displaying her cleavage. She said, "I'm here for the Crown Prince's wedding party. But before I do my act, I want to know what kind of place this is. There's some guy who's a duke who wants to see me—is he okay?"

She went on with that sort of talk for some time. I was mesmerized, but finally asked her to describe just what kind of act she planned. "I dance," she said, and I tried not to imagine what sort of dance she might do. She asked if I were going to the feast. "Yes, we were invited," I said. "Well," she said, "I've got two big ostrich feather fans, and three roses, and that's my costume." I thought to myself, "Saints, preserve us!"

The woman's name, she firmly advised me, was Charlene Chastle—as in chaste, not castle. She was really was something else. She told me that in Rome she had taken off all her clothes and climbed into the Trevi fountain. In Algeria she'd been kidnapped by the Bedouins, and in Cairo she had posed in front of the Sphinx with her fans. She recounted her whole life story. I took it in and then warned her, "You know, this is a very different country. The people here are not used to some things that people in the U.S. or Europe might enjoy." I was trying to get her to understand that Ethiopia was an entirely different culture, one where her usual stunts might not be appreciated. She seemed to listen to my admonitions.

The following night Ms. Chastle appeared at the banquet. The entertainment began. A gilded Egyptian man demonstrated how he could move his muscles independently of each other, rippling them wildly, then a French fellow juggled. Then Charlene did her fan dance—and it knocked everybody for a loop. People were absolutely dumbfounded by this vaudeville fan dancer. She did indeed create a sensation.

The next day was Timkat, a very holy day for Ethiopians, who are Orthodox Christians. Each year on Timkat, the Emperor and the nobility are re-baptized. They set up a long pool, along which many priests stood with decorated umbrellas and tinkling bells. It was an awesome scene, resplendent with formality.

We were lined up, waiting respectfully for the ceremony to begin, when I looked across the pool and, lo and behold, who should appear but the blonde bombshell herself! We stood as the emperor arrived. As the third secretary in the German embassy, Gerhard Fischer, rose from his seat, the fan dancer climbed up on his chair, put her elbows on his shoulders and rested her camera on his head to take photographs. Everybody could see this. They were thunderstruck that anyone could act with such audacity at so solemn an affair. Thankfully Ms. Chastle did not jump into the pool, as I, in a wave of panic, feared she might.

When it was all over, I went back to the embassy and, for laughs, wrote a report on the Blonde Bombshell, as I called her. I sent it to the Ambassador as a joke, but he transmitted it to the State Department, without my knowledge. Later I received a note from Secretary of State John Foster Dulles, saying, "I applaud your dispatch." He was a very dour person. I don't think anyone ever saw him smile, so, coming from him, this expression of delight was remarkable, although it was a rather odd way to impress my highest boss. Another high official wrote a more whimsical critique of my memo.

My dispatch about the fan dancer was distributed throughout the Foreign Service. For a long time, officers from all over the world reminded me of my report. It, along with a photograph of the Blonde Bombshell, is among my papers.

While in Ethiopia, I resolved to fulfill a childhood dream. As a boy, I collected foreign stamps and read books by explorers. Richard Halliburton was my favorite, but the British explorer Sir Richard Burton, who wrote about his quest to find the source of the Blue Nile, also made an impression on me. The White Nile, they had discovered, originates in Lake Victoria, but no one was sure where the Blue Nile came from. Burton finally discovered its origin.

I set out to retrace Burton's steps to the source of the Blue Nile. By this time I was a father and Dolores was again pregnant, so she could not come with me. I hitched a ride on a plane that brought me near the western end of Lake Tana in Ethiopia. There I paid a native boatman a few cents to transport me on a boat made of long reeds. We rode the bundled reeds like a horse, with our feet dangling on both sides. Oddly, the tribesmen used slender bamboo poles as paddles, which wasn't a terribly efficient way to travel. The fact that our feet were dragging in the water didn't help. Eventually, however, we arrived at the point where the lake overflows in cascades—the beginning of the Blue Nile. I thought to myself, "Well, there are not many New Mexicans who have done this!" I had followed the footsteps of a childhood hero. I felt very much the world explorer.

When we arrived back to camp after re-crossing the lake, the boatman speared some fish for dinner. As we prepared to cook them over a fire, we found they contained masses of worms or leeches, attached to their innards. I wouldn't eat them. In talking around the fire, the natives informed me that the lake was home to crocodiles. I shuddered to think that I had crossed the lake with my feet hanging down in the water.

We left Ethiopia with two children in tow, stopping on our way to our next posting to visit Dolores's parents in Washington. My children were so used to being around black people that they went directly to any black person we encountered. At the building where my in-laws lived, Tina always held the black elevator operator's hand.

After Washington, I brought Dolores to Santa Fe for her first visit. Everybody in the family was delighted to meet her, and she loved what she saw.

The novice diplomat on his first mission to the Sudan
with Sayed Abdul Rahman al Mahdi, 1952

I acquire a lifetime partner May 2, 1953

Received in the Court of His Imperial Majesty Emperor Haile Selassie, King of Kings, Conquering Lion of Judah, Addis Ababa, 1953

Ethiopian horsemen

Miss Charlene Chastle tours Africa, 1955

Exploring an
Underground Church
Lalibela, Ethiopia

A childhood dream fulfilled.
Visiting the source of the Blue Nile, Ethiopia, 1954

The source of the Blue Nile.

Three of the kids at the ranch becoming Americanized

5

Mexico City the First Time Around: A Prideful Mistake

When we arrived in Mexico City in 1955 with two kids, I was well known in the Foreign Service because of my fan dancer report. We were received "with interest," you might say. The Ambassador first assigned me to the economic section, but as a bilingual with political experience, I was moved to the political section almost immediately. I did pretty well. Within a short time, Dolores and I were accepted in those circles that were important to U.S. interests. My immediate boss, Andrew Donovan, was of the old school, and very demanding. I couldn't get away with doing things half-way, which was very good for my training.

The U.S. Ambassador to Mexico at the time, Francis White, of an old Baltimore family also was tough—so much so that he was scary. He rarely smiled and was very rigid. He intimidated me and gave me the impression that he thought of me as an unlettered dolt. Then, strangely enough, he started inviting Dolores and me to important dinners and events at the embassy. He saw we could interact easily with his most important and sophisticated guests. When he left Mexico at the end of his tenure there, he wrote a letter to the Director General of the Foreign Service commending me as a very good officer. He recommended that the Service give me good assignments. I was surprised when I received a copy of his letter and the Director General's favorable reply.

Ambassador White was replaced by Robert C. Hill, from New Hampshire, a very rich man, high in Republican circles whose impatience made him a bull in a china closet. He immediately took me out of the political section and made me his special assistant. This required a very close relationship.

I had some peculiar problems working with Hill. For example, he had the habit of sending me off to buy things without providing me with the money to do so. As my expenses started to add up, I asked if we could start a petty cash fund. Hill reacted angrily, demanding to know why I needed money. When I explained that neither the Embassy nor I pay his petty expenses, he was surprised. The upshot of this and other interactions was that Hill respected me for speaking up, and our relationship improved. He was not used to having people stand up to him and I was not about to be subservient to anyone.

Mexico in the 1950s was still very much under the political, economic, and cultural dominance of the autocratic, statist *Partido Revolucionario Institucional* (PRI). Mexicans accepted rampant corruption as a fact of life, and basic economic and political precepts that we universally hold in the U.S. were mostly anathema to the governing circles of Mexico. I brashly coined a new motto for the PRI: "Don't rock the trough." The slogan was published in a Drew Pearson newspaper column, but fortunately was not attributed to me.

These fundamental differences in governance and economics made U.S.-Mexican relations very difficult at the time. The U.S. embassy worked hard to improve the situation but seemed to be content with just holding the line.

After a short time, leading Mexicans came to like my family and me and invited us to many social and official gatherings. This was not always the case with other embassy officers. As was our habit, we reciprocated by inviting people to our home often. We also joined a club for junior diplomats, which further put us in contact with diplomats from other countries. Ironically, our very success in making significant contacts created a major problem for me.

One fine day, the CIA station chief called me to his office and asked if I would help his agency. He knew of our success in getting officials to come to our home. The CIA was actively recruiting agents and at that time was particularly interested in some junior diplomatic officers of various embassies in Mexico City. He told me that the CIA could provide me with money if I would entertain certain people at our home. The idea was that we would also invite CIA officers to our gatherings so they could pursue intelligence interests. This was in 1956, in the thick of the Cold War, and recruiting spies and/or moles was widespread.

I told the station chief I wasn't sure I should do that sort of thing. He appealed to my patriotism, saying, "Aren't you here to help your country? Nobody else in the embassy has your contacts." He suggested that if I didn't cooperate, we would lose an opportunity to glean valuable intelligence. As an impressionable young officer, I agreed to host the gatherings out of a sense of duty.

For the next six or seven months, the CIA subsidized our social events. Like most diplomats in the Foreign Service, I was already receiving an entertainment allowance, but, as Second Secretary, I received only $100 a year, in four quarterly payments. With $25 a quarter, we couldn't entertain much. Fortunately, Dolores was able to work wonders. She discovered that most foreigners in Mexico had never eaten peanut butter. A canapé of peanut butter with a bit of bacon delighted them almost as much as the finest Russian caviar. When the peanut butter canapés came out at our cocktail parties, the foreigners pounced upon them, chasing them down with cheap liquor from the commissary. Dolores had many such tricks that made our parties inexpensive but unique.

The extra money from the CIA allowed us to host more and better social events. As instructed, I invited people of interest to the CIA. After about six months, the CIA called me in again to express their amazement at the success of our arrangement. They thought the number two officer in the Russian embassy, Boris Kazantsev, was ready to become a U.S. agent. I enthusiastically said, "Gosh. That is amazing." "But to get him to come over to our side," they continued, "we need your help." I protested that I had only met him a couple of times. They came back with, "Yes, we know, but he will come to your house if you invite him." So I agreed to invite him over. "And who else should I invite?" I asked. "We want you to invite Kazantsev alone," they said. "It will be just the two of you." Of course, I was impressed; I would handle this assignment by myself. It didn't take much more cajoling to talk me into aiming for a major patriotic achievement.

I invited Minister Kazantsev for lunch and he accepted. As directed, I had given our maid the day off and sent the children off with Dolores so I would be alone with Kazantsev. Our house on Monte Ararat was a large bungalow with a garage and maid's quarters in the basement. The CIA planted an agent in the basement and wired the house, placing listening devices under the tables and other places. My instructions were clear: during lunch, I was to ask Kazantsev if he would be willing to work for the U.S. I was to say that it would bring happiness to both of our countries if he were to work with us. I wouldn't discuss how much money the CIA would give him; my task was simply to see if he would agree to be a U.S. agent.

I was foolish to acquiesce to the CIA's request. My superiors in the embassy knew of my extracurricular activities but never warned me about the possible ramifications. They seemed proud of me. I was only a second secretary at the embassy, but the CIA people inflated my ego, saying things like, "Nobody else can do this," and, "Everybody loves you." I believed it!

I invited Boris for lunch—and the CIA had made sure that it was a very good lunch, cooked and served by one of their maids. I gave Kazantsev Dvorak's *New World Symphony,* because he had told me he loved music. He was very touched. We proceeded to enjoy a pleasant lunch, while the technician in the basement listened to and taped our conversation. I was very nervous. I had been told not to drink much until dessert was served and to be sure to ask Kazantsev about his family. He told me about his daughter and two sons who were in technical schools in the Soviet Union, doing very well and studying hard. His bosses wouldn't let his family come to Mexico, he said.

The friendly conversation went on like this for some time before I finally got down to the big question: "You know, sir, we're aware that you don't comport with a lot of things that go on in your country and that you would like to change them." There was stony silence from him, but I went on. "A lot of good Russian people are working to change things. From what I know about you, I thought maybe you'd be ready to join their efforts to change things." He asked me, "What do you mean?"

"Why don't you come with us?" I suggested "You can stay with your present position. We'll put a sympathetic handler to work with you and every so often you can tell us what it is we can do together to bring about change in your country." After another uncomfortable silence Kazantsev said, "This has been a fine lunch. Thank you." And off he went. I knew my effort had not worked. He had not been responsive at all. As if to confirm this, the next day he sent back the *New World Symphony.*

I reported to the CIA station chief that I had blown it and that I was no good at recruitment. I suggested he find someone better at that kind of business. With that, I assumed the whole business was concluded, but the episode was to have serious and long-lasting consequences for me. The unforeseen end result was that I was placed on the Soviet KGB's list of dangerous American intelligence agents. That classification followed me throughout my career. My error in judgment, susceptibility to flattery, and overconfidence made me a prime target for the Soviet KGB.

The repercussions were numerous and pernicious. In Peru in 1969 the government accused me, as "Latin American head of the CIA," of leading a plot to assassinate the president of that country, and I was given hours to leave Peru. I refused and survived the ensuing clash between the Peruvian and U.S. governments. In Grenada, I was again attacked as the leader of a plan to overthrow Bishop's Marxist government. These and similar charges were made in most of the countries where I served, all because of my fabricated reputation as a senior CIA operative. The Communist press printed lurid attacks on me at every turn. Radios Moscow and Havana made broadcasts cataloguing my alleged nefarious activities on a regular basis.

My amateurish recruitment flop in Mexico assured that the leftist press in every country in which I served attacked me as dangerous and identified me as the head of the CIA in Latin America. All this unmerited hostile attention only made me more appreciated and admired by the majority democratic elements of the countries in which I served, so I was actually helped more than damaged by the otherwise troubling attacks. However, I was more than fascinated to find myself a target for leftist elements in the U.S. as well. Some of these attacks came from individuals having important positions in the American media. Karen de Young of the *Washington Post,* Michael Massing in the *Atlantic Monthly,* and Larry Birns of the Americas Watch Committee published accusatory and untrue attacks—and I responded. My challenge prompted an extraordinary, several-column apology and retraction by the *Washington Post.*[1]

Furthermore, I was given access to the pages of the *Atlantic Monthly*[2], the editors of which became very accommodating of me. *Newsweek* magazine did a cover story entitled "The KGB in America,"[3] which featured me as an American official who had been specifically targeted by Soviet intelligence. That was no surprise to me; I, after more than twenty years, had no doubt at all that I was a prime KGB target.[4]

My alleged CIA eminence also led to accusations of responsibility whenever Soviets defected to the West and I was anywhere nearby. In Buenos Aires, for example, four trapeze artists from the Russian circus decided to defect. They came to our embassy seeking asylum, which was granted. The Russian Ambassador was furious, certain that I had orchestrated their defection, even though I had nothing to do with it. Accusations like that dogged me all the rest of my career. There are still some who believe I'm with the CIA.

Strangely enough, the belief that I was an important CIA operative probably protected me throughout my career. Some people

---

1. *Washington Post,* January 7, 1981
2. *Atlantic Monthly,* February 1984 and June 1984
3. *Newsweek,* November 23, 1981
4. I especially treasure my file on my exchanges with the *Post* and the *Monthly.* Those publications and others relating to events cited in this book are available at the Fray Angélico Chávez History Library in Santa Fe, which is the repository of my papers.

thought me powerful, dangerous, and capable of dark acts or even of contracting assassinations. Enemies didn't openly confront me. If they'd taken me just for who I really was—a common, ordinary diplomat—I may well have been kidnapped or murdered early on. I apparently had an air of mystery and power about me. I remember the East German Ambassador once saying to me, "You're doing a good job." I said, "Well, thank you. I try." To which he replied, "No, the covert job you're doing so very well." I said, "What covert job?" "You know what I mean," he said slyly.

The exaggerated title of senior CIA agent all began with Boris Kazantsev, who later became the Russian Ambassador to Cuba and much later defected to the West. I personally never saw him or heard from him again.

More important than my mythical status as a CIA operative, my performance evaluations ranked me number two in my class of officers when my assignment in Mexico ended after two years. I was flattered to be included in "Who's Who in America," but my status did me no good when it came time to register my son's birth: I could not persuade the Mexican birth certificate official to permit me to name my second son "Hernán," a name that is anathema to many Mexicans because of Hernán Cortes's legacy as conqueror of Mexico.

Ambassador Hill asked me to extend my tour of duty. We loved Mexico, so I did agree to stay, but the State Department informed me that I couldn't because the Undersecretary of State wanted me to work for him in Washington. We began packing to return to our nation's capital.

6

In the Heart of the State Department

The Undersecretary of State, Christian Herter, who was my new boss in the State Department, was a former Governor of Massachusetts and a gentleman of the old school. President Eisenhower had created the Operations Coordinating Board as an action arm of the White House. The board was comprised of the undersecretaries of key departments and the heads of other agencies. The Board's primary responsibility was to oversee the implementation of the foreign policies determined by the National Security Council and approved by the President.

Every week I'd attend the OCB meetings as a State Department action officer. Sometimes I was assigned special tasks. Our positions on the board gave us great access and authority. We conveyed the decisions of the White House regarding policies and their implementation directly to the appropriate agencies. If the President approved an NSC decision to begin negotiations for foreign military base rights, for example, I would communicate the specific instructions and determine a timetable and its compliance. The job put me at the center of executive power in Washington during a very critical time. It gave me access at the highest levels into the White House and federal agencies. It was a most amazing, wonderful position for a junior officer.

I served with the OCB for two years. It was a heady time, but not without its challenges. Once, about the time that radical young military officers were becoming a factor in Libya, the President asked for a memo on what was going on in that country. I had a role in the preparation of the memo. Eisenhower would only read one-page memos, so we sent him a summary on the situation in Libya. Foolishly, we wrote that King Idris was seventy years old and definitely "over the hill." We said that the king could not be expected to last much longer and that the young colonels were going to take over the country. The President sent the memo back with a note: "Surely you know that I'll be seventy soon." I was terribly embarrassed.

One particular event during my time at the Operations Coordinating Board made a profound impression on me. I was informed that I would be leaving the city for a day. I was not to tell anyone—not even my wife—where I was going and was required to sign a form obligating me not to reveal what I was to see. A bit puzzled, I put together a travel kit and told Dolores that the State Department was sending me on a field exercise.

The next morning, a van collected me and several others and we drove towards Thurmond, Maryland, which is very close to Camp David, the President's retreat. The road we were following, a rather wide, well-paved thoroughfare, led directly into a tunnel in the side of a mountain. We paused at heavy steel gates that sealed the tunnel's entrance. The doors slid back and we entered. The road curved and then we came to another heavy steel door. When we stopped we found ourselves in an underground warren of passageways.

In due time we learned the purpose of this extraordinary trip. Because of our jobs and our knowledge, we had been chosen to be that part of the American government that would take control of the country's foreign policy if a nuclear attack destroyed Washington, D.C. If nuclear war came to pass, this underground labyrinth would be our safe refuge, because no nuclear weapon then extant could penetrate the mountain.

During the orientation we were shown a list of the primary Soviet missile targets in the United States, according to U.S. intelligence sources. Washington was very close to the top of the list, of course, but to my horror I saw that specific sites in New Mexico were there also. I was stunned.

The orientation revealed a chilling scenario: if there were any indication of an imminent missile strike, we would be contacted immediately and told to gather at a designated site. From there, we'd be flown by helicopter to Thurmond to go immediately underground. Once ensconced in our fortress, we would function as best we could to direct the foreign policy of the United States government. Congress had the same sort of bunker out in West Virginia, where the surviving congressional leadership would take shelter and try to resurrect a government.

The tour leader showed me to the part of the cave I would share with another person. It included bunk beds and the most basic supplies, and off to one side was a small office. I couldn't quite figure out how we were going to be effective from deep in that cave, although sophisticated radio equipment was supposed to keep us in communication with whomever was left on the surface.

Those of us chosen to be survivors and government leaders in the event of a nuclear holocaust felt in some ways honored—until the question was asked, "Where do our families go?" There was a silence and then we were informed that there was no place in the shelter for our family members. We would have to go alone, leaving our loved ones to fend for themselves on the surface. That made the deepest impression on me and vastly increased my fears about the consequences of nuclear war, not only to our country but to the whole world of families and friends. I wasn't sure my strong sense of duty and responsibility would carry me through such a situation. Contemplating the frightening possibilities served to deepen my religious faith.

The election of 1960 brought John Kennedy to power. Soon after his inauguration, he moved to abolish the Operations Coordinating Board. He did not believe in a structured, hierarchical administration; instead he said he wanted "constructive conflict" in his administration. In effect my wonderful job was abolished. Thomas Mann, whom I knew well, became the new Assistant Secretary for Inter-American

Affairs. Thomas Mann played a big role in my career. I had my greatest single success in the Foreign Service while working under him. I'd first met him at the party where I first met Dolores, and he remembered us. When, in 1953, Dolores and I were on a ship bound for Africa, he and his wife were also aboard. Seven years after that voyage, I went to work as a special assistant for Mann when he became Assistant Secretary for Inter-American Affairs,

Unknown to me, Mann was already involved in super secret planning for the Bay of Pigs invasion of Cuba. This disaster happened shortly after I began working for him. He had managed to keep the secret from me. I knew nothing about the planned invasion before the events unfolded. The President had named Adolphe Berle as one of a team to help oversee the Bay of Pigs invasion. Berle and Richard Helms of the CIA finished the final planning for the operation. Strangely enough, the Operations Coordinating Board, which also approved covert actions, was involved in executing the policy decision to invade Cuba. But even though I worked with the Board, the plan was so secret that I didn't know about it even then.

I missed out on the planning of the invasion, but I was there for its disastrous outcomes. I remember very vividly the night that everything fell apart. A gathering that night at Adolphe Berle's house was like a funeral—everybody was shaking their heads in disbelief and shock.

After the massive foreign policy failure of the Bay of Pigs invasion, President Kennedy felt guilty—and rightly so. After all, he sent exiled Cubans into Cuba without air support, and they were easily defeated. Kennedy's guilt led to his determination to secure the release of the Cuban exiles that Castro imprisoned. Some very rich Kennedy supporters from Tennessee were negotiating with the Cuban government for the release of the prisoners. The Cubans were demanding a sizable ransom, but the President was emphatic that the U.S. would not pay them a money ransom. Instead, he offered Castro medicines and commodities. The White House called to confirm that I spoke fluent Spanish, which led to my involvement in negotiating with the Cubans through the mediation of the International Red Cross. In the end, Castro released most of the prisoners—in exchange for twenty or thirty million dollars worth of medicine and medical supplies, wheat flour, and other foodstuffs. My participation in the negotiations gave me valuable experience with high level bargaining.

President Kennedy embarked on the Alliance for Progress as a new opening to Latin America, while I was working in the front office of the Inter-American bureau. Occasionally, before bureaucratic obstacles had gelled, Kennedy relied on me for specific information on Latin America. The phone would ring, I'd pick it up and in his Boston accent he would say something like, "It's John Kennedy here. What's the name of the President of Costa Rica?" Those occasional contacts with the White House heightened the heavy work load I carried.

Kennedy had an unlovable advisor, Dick Goodwin, who wrote speeches for him. This speechwriter called one day when I was working late. He was at home writing a speech for the President and needed x, y, z and w right away. I said I'd get the material to him as soon as I was able to close up the office and leave. He said, "I want it now." I said I was sorry, but I was in charge of the office and there was nobody else to take care of things. I told him I would get the documents and drop them off just as soon as I could.

When I finished work, I hitched a ride in the pouring rain with Jamie Jamison to Goodwin's address. We parked the car near steep steps that led up to the front door. I ran up in the rain to huddle in a small portal and ring the doorbell. The Persian blinds parted and a bleary eye peeked out at me. The door opened to reveal the speechwriter in rumpled pajamas, unshaven, and smelling bad. I looked past him into the house to see utter chaos. There was a mattress on the floor, papers lying everywhere. It was a repellent sight. He glared at me and said, "God damn it, it's about time!" He ripped the papers from my hand and slammed the door in my face. I fell down the concrete steps and fractured my arm.

I was stunned and in pain as I lay in the rain. My colleague who had driven me there didn't see me fall, so he didn't come to help me. Eventually, a driver for the White House came to deliver something else to the house. He saw me lying in the rain and asked if I was all right. I replied that I was not sure. He helped me to our car and Jamie drove me home. I slept painfully on the fractured arm that night.

That was Dick Goodwin for you. He never tried to help me, and he never apologized for the incident. Years later, in an article in the *New Yorker* about the International Petroleum Company case in Peru, he criticized me on what seemed to me to be a pretext.

While I was dealing with the heavy duty professional responsibilities in Washington during those years, my last son, James, was born, on November 24, 1960—on exactly the day, in the same hospital and on the same floor where Jacqueline Kennedy was giving birth to John-John. Poor Dolores was more or less ignored by the doctors and nursing staff, who had no time for her. To see my wife and child I had to be frisked by the Secret Service and escorted up the elevator.

My time at the State Department in those years was a profound learning experience for me. Still, I was glad when Tom Mann asked me join him in Mexico later that year, where he would assume the ambassadorship. He said he needed me for a special task. I was glad to leave the Kennedy scene. I never quite adjusted to the ego-driven arrogance and posturing then running rampant in Washington. I leapt at the offer to return to dear old Mexico. Dolores looked forward to finding good help with our four rambunctious children.

7

Mexico for a Second Time: A Successful Negotiation

Not much had changed in Mexico in the three years we had been away. There was a pleasant new president, but the autocratic, corrupt, statist system still prevailed. My special task in Mexico the second time around involved a serious, longstanding border dispute. Ambassador Mann believed that if we failed to solve this problem it would permanently damage our relations with Mexico. Resolving the issue became my number one priority.

The situation had come about because of a shift in the course of the Rio Grande in 1863 that cut off a largish chunk of Mexican territory and placed it on the United States side of the river. The Mexicans wanted it back, but it wasn't so simple to execute a transfer, since the land in question was soon developed as part of downtown El Paso, Texas. Through decades of contention, the U.S. had consistently refused to return the parcel. The two governments finally agreed to arbitration by an international tribunal, headed by a Canadian. The tribunal's decision in favor of Mexico in 1909 directed the United States to return the land, but by then American interests had been building on it for 40 years and the U.S. ignored the tribunal's finding—a position our enemies in Mexico never stopped trumpeting.

The disputed real estate was called the Chamizal. When I was given the assignment, I was told that if the problem wasn't solved very soon, the solution would never happen and the damage to bilateral relations would be permanent. I pointed out to Ambassador Mann that, as a second secretary, I lacked the clout to negotiate with high level Mexican officials and American business and political leaders involved with the issue. I was concerned that no one would take me seriously. The Ambassador acknowledged my handicap but still wanted me to do the job. He flew with me to El Paso to help me establish relationships with the real sources of power in the region. We met with Samuel Young, a very powerful owner of one of the biggest banks and companies in El Paso, and several others, telling them that settling the dispute would probably involve transferring de facto U.S. territory back to Mexican ownership. We asked for their support in our endeavor. Young promised his support but admonished us, "For God's sake, keep it secret until we have a deal, because if it gets out that we're talking about giving land to Mexico, you'll never get away with it."

From El Paso, the Ambassador and I flew to Austin to meet with Governor John Connelly, who was in the hospital with a hernia. At a meeting around his hospital bed, he said he would support us but agreed that we should keep the negotiations secret. We continued on to Houston, where we obtained assurances of backing from other power brokers, including the publisher of the *Houston Post,* a man named Hobby. Vice President Lyndon Johnson also endorsed our endeavor. Again, the consensus was that we should not make anything public until we were sure we would be successful.

With access to these powerful mentors, I spent a couple of years working on the Chamizal settlement. I traveled back and forth between El Paso, Washington, and Mexico City, working closely with Joe Friedkin of the International Border and Water Commission. We began meeting secretly with the Mexicans. My primary contact in Mexico was Vicente Sanchez Gavito, who was already an Ambassador. Sanchez Gavito and I got along well, although initially to get something to him I had to go through the Mexican Foreign Minister Manuel Tello. I acquired a stack of Esso maps of downtown El Paso to use during negotiations. I'd draw a line on a map, suggesting that the U.S. could pass to Mexico a certain portion of land. The Mexicans would look it over and come back with a counter offer, and so forth. These were strictly informal discussions that we could always deny having, especially since all the proposals were on unofficial maps.[5]

The proposals and counter-proposals went to the foreign minister through Pepe Gallastegui, a guy my age who was very helpful. We began making progress and after a while it began to look as if we were going to reach agreement. As time went on, I assumed responsibility for drafting the agreements, with the help of an assistant and a brilliant woman in the legal section of the State Department, Marjorie Whitman.

Finally, after almost two years of work, I had a text that the Mexicans were happy with. It specified that the U.S. would cut a certain number of acres of land from U.S. territory, mostly in the Chamizal, and return them to Mexico, while Mexico would agree to give up some acreage in the Chamizal and some adjacent land. Mexico would end up with the exact number of acres it had always demanded. The settlement also required the nations to re-channel the Rio Grande, deepen it, and line it with concrete. The final price tag was about $40 million. It was a remarkable resolution of a complex problem. The Ambassador was very pleased with my work.

President Kennedy then decided to make a state visit to Mexico City to get a firm commitment from the Mexican president on the Chamizal settlement. I was in charge of organizing the visit. I recommended that the Kennedys attend mass at the Basilica of Guadalupe in Mexico City, but the Ambassador argued that having the president attend mass would open old church-state wounds in Mexico. While he was correct that Mexican law specifically prohibited the president of Mexico from going into a church, I argued that it didn't matter if the Mexican president went or not; if Kennedy went, he would win over the people of Mexico. In

5. The Chamizal National Memorial Museum in El Paso contains many of my papers and photographs relating to the settlement of the treaty, including the original, definitive Esso map.

the end, I prevailed and the President and Mrs. Kennedy attended Mass at the Basilica. Massive crowds cheered them. Afterwards, on the suggestion of the military attaché, Kennedy laid a wreath at the monument to the *Niños Héroes*—the site where Mexican cadets had died at Chapultepec while defending the capital from U.S. forces in 1847. The whole country of Mexico then went wild in their acclaim for Kennedy. (In arranging the Kennedys' luncheon for the Mexican President, I went back and forth with Tish Baldridge in the White House. When I complained that she was bringing too little California red wine, she floored me by telling me not to serve it in beer steins!)

Kennedy used his visit to announce that agreement to the terms of the Chamizal settlement had been reached. It seemed this long festering problem was coming to resolution. Previously, I had briefed appropriate members of the U.S. Senate. We needed Senate ratification of the treaty, which called for the U.S. to cede schools, houses, and other structures to Mexico, along with the land. We arranged to compensate U.S. citizens who lost property, even though they had dubious legal title. Senator Ralph Yarborough from Texas was firmly behind the treaty, but Texas' other senator, John Tower, was strongly opposed.

Senator Tower, like all the senators, was pledged to confidentiality, but he desperately wanted to leak the story to the press. Whenever I'd go to his office to brief him, he would unleash on me a terrorizing Texas newspaper woman named Sarah McClenden. She was a real vixen. Quietly, he'd summon her to try to drag out of me the details of the Chamizal treaty so she could attack it. The first time this happened, I was hard pressed to fend her off. The next time she cornered me, I simply retreated to the men's room and waited there until they told me the senator would see me.

Tower held the view that the disputed land was United States territory—and "sacred" Texas soil to boot. He believed after 100 years of occupation the U.S. legally owned it. He made it clear that he didn't give a damn what the international tribunal said and warned that if we tried to give it away, he was going to raise hell.

As we sought to garner the support of Tower and other senators, I considered myself in an awkward position. As I reminded Ambassador

Mann, Texas and New Mexico had a history of enmity and disputed land claims between them. It might not set well with Tower and other Texans to have a New Mexican named Ortiz giving Texas soil to Mexico. To make sure this aspect didn't hit the fan and undermine support for the treaty, I asked Ambassador Mann for a transfer away from Mexico. He responded by pointing out that I had already done all the basic work and there had been no ethnic attacks. He thought I was being overly sensitive. Finally, though, I prevailed and was transferred to Washington to work on Spanish issues. The Chamizal treaty sailed through the Senate with Tower casting the only vote against it, so I was wrong.

The Mexican government fully appreciated my work on the Chamizal treaty and awarded me two large gold medals for my efforts. President Johnson gave me a silver medal. Those involved in the treaty settlement knew that I had made the major effort to draft it and see it through. My success brought me recognition in the State Department and the Foreign Service. I received the Superior Honor award and other recognition at big ceremonies. My fan dancer fame faded beside my new reputation as a negotiator and peacemaker—closer to the mark of what I had hoped to accomplish in the Service.

While serving in Mexico, I by chance became peripherally involved in the terrifying nuclear standoff over the Cuban Missile Crisis, which unfolded in October of 1962. The Secretary of the Treasury, Douglas Dillon, was in Mexico City for a meeting with the Ministers of Finance of all the Latin American countries (except Cuba) to talk about Kennedy's Alliance for Progress. He was there to discuss the parameters of the program and the United States' plans for strengthening economic development in the hemisphere.

Ambassador Mann was attending the ceremonies in the ballroom of the Maria Isabel Hotel. I stayed in the office to work on papers. We had heard the news that the United States had declared a preemptive naval blockade of Cuba in response to the discovery of Soviet missiles there. The line had been drawn, and Kennedy had declared that the U.S. would sink any ship that tried to cross it. We knew that U.S. armed forces were on full alert and that Kennedy was on the verge of calling up the reserves. American soldiers occupied the beaches of

Florida as Russian ships loaded with missiles headed toward the embargo line. The question was, if they didn't stop, would Kennedy sink them? Who would blink first, Khrushchev or Kennedy? It was a very tense and scary situation.

All this was developing quickly, while the Ambassador was away from the embassy. I was sitting at my desk when the code clerk approached me, almost trembling, holding a message. "This has come in. The Ambassador must read it right away," he said. He went on to stipulate that the Ambassador was not to take notes and that he must burn the message after reading it. The clerk was ordered to make a record of everyone who saw the cable and certify its destruction. Regulations specified that only the clerk and the Ambassador were to see the note, but the clerk said to me, "I know he shows you everything, and I want to get rid of it!" He dropped the message on my desk and departed.

As I read the cable, the space around me seemed to whirl. It was addressed to President López Mateos from President John Kennedy. I don't believe the contents of that message have ever been revealed. I have never said much about it before and will not disclose the full, unbelievable contents.

The essence of the message was that within hours there could be a nuclear war between the Soviet Union and the United States. Given this dire circumstance, Kennedy asked for López Mateos to provide assurances that he would respond favorably to several explicit demands. Kennedy noted that it was a certainty that great numbers of Mexican citizens would be killed by the USSR's nuclear attack because some of the primary U.S. targets lay along the border. He said that the U.S. government would have no way of stopping a mass exodus of American refugees into Mexico and that, to ensure that they would not become an undue burden on the Mexican government's resources, a transfer would be made of U.S. assets to Mexico. Kennedy went on to request an immediate guarantee that the U.S. would have access to Mexican military facilities if they were needed.

The message effectively stated that Kennedy expected the prompt and total support of the Mexican government. I read it over and thought the end was near. We had very little time to take action, but the Ambassador was attending a formal ceremony on the stage of the hotel ballroom and the president of Mexico was over the Pacific, returning from a state visit to the Philippines. While he was out of the country, the Minister of the Interior acted as Mexico's Chief Executive. At that time, the minister was Diaz Ordaz, a wiry, smart Zapotec Indian with mahogany colored skin. I called Diaz Ordaz's executive secretary, Luis Farias, and said, "Luis, it's going to take me about 15 minutes to get Ambassador Mann. I will bring him over to see the minister immediately." Luis responded that he'd try and fit us in the next day. "He's briefing the governors of five states and he's not available," he said. "Luis," I said, "I'm not asking if we can see him. I'm telling you, we're going to see him." "Who in the hell do you think you are?" he asked. I simply told him I was going to get the Ambassador and that we were on our way. As I was hanging up, I heard Luis ask, "*¿Estás loco?* (Have you gone mad?)"

I rushed to the hotel and told the driver not to move, that I would bring the Ambassador out. I ran into the hotel and without hesitating marched past everybody in the ballroom and up onto the stage. I said to the Ambassador, "Sir, we're leaving now to see Diaz Ordaz." He said, "What are you doing here?" and told me to get off the stage. I looked him in the eye and said, "Sir, we have to go immediately." He could tell something serious was up, but he said, "This better be important or I'm going to kick your butt!" He advised Secretary Dillon that an emergency required him to leave, and we left. Those in the hall wondered what was going on.

I showed Ambassador Mann the cable in the car. He shook his head and said, "Oh, my Lord." We arrived at the Ministry of the Interior. Luis Farias had pulled the minister out of his meeting with the governors. The minister was obviously annoyed, but we didn't bother with the niceties when we came in—no "good day, how are you, sorry to bother you," or anything like that. Mann said, "We have an urgent message for President López Mateos. We know he's away but we can help you contact him. We need an immediate answer from him, and the answer has to be positive."

We read the message to Diaz Ordaz, because we couldn't give him a copy, and even that mahogany skin turned pale. Amazingly, his immediate response was, "I don't have to contact the president of Mexico. It's not necessary for me to get his approval for what you ask of us. When you gringos put your balls on the table," he slapped his desk, "we're with you. Tell Kennedy that!" Ambassador Mann replied that, with all due respect, our government wanted the personal assurances of López Mateos. Diaz Ordaz said, "Damn it, I told you, I'm in charge here when he's gone and that's it!"

The Ambassador and I went back to the embassy, burned the incoming message and reported to Washington on what we'd heard. We weren't sure how it was going to be received. The response of the White House is noted in a 1997 book, *The Kennedy Tapes.* Kennedy, who wasn't happy that Ambassador Mann hadn't heard directly from López Mateos, managed to find a way to contact his Mexican colleague over Hawaii.

I was shaken by the whole episode. My family commented on how exceptionally loving and affectionate I was that night.

I later learned that Ambassadors in several countries had received similar doomsday messages from Kennedy. I've come to wonder if the messages might have been a ruse—that Kennedy intended that the Russian embassies quickly learn of them and believe that the U.S. was really ready for war. It was expected this would cause the Russians to back down. In any case, something worked, because the Russian ship that was coming towards our warships off Cuba stopped and turned back. The standoff was over. We know now that Kennedy had agreed secretly to a pledge that the U.S. would never invade Cuba and that we would withdraw our Jupiter missiles from Turkey. Kennedy never admitted that deal, but in the final hour an agreement was made that apparently saved us from the ultimate holocaust. To me, that was Kennedy's greatest accomplishment.

On one of my last days in Mexico I received a gratifying farewell call from Augustín Salvat, the head of the ruling party's Institute of Political and Economic Studies, a very influential Mexican political institution. Early on, Ambassador Mann had assigned me the task of trying to persuade the prominent Institute to include in its core programs state policies such as a free market, free press, democratic election procedures, free exchange of ideas and other democratic concepts. This was a very tough task, since the Institute's instructors were almost all statists or Marxists. Finally I succeeded in having a couple of Spanish-speaking American political scientists and economists give lectures at the Institute. We also gave several of the Mexican students and instructors all-expenses-paid tours of the U.S. I doubted we had made much of a dent in the ruling party's destructive ideology, but I felt good about establishing excellent personal relationships with PRI leaders.

I was pleasantly surprised when Salvat, in his farewell to me, said I deserved to know that the previous evening the PRI's Central Committee had voted to change a basic party precept. Henceforth, the PRI declared, in Mexico it was "licit to make a profit!!" Since Salvat had a monopoly on the importation of Dairy Queen soft ice cream machines and was a very rich man, the about-face in official ideology was not changing reality for him and many other Mexican businessmen all that much. Nevertheless, I was touched by his giving me credit for helping persuade the PRI to change a core canon.

8

A Time of Transition in Spain—Department of State

The Cuban Missile crisis gave me some of the most dramatic moments in my career, but of more enduring substance for me was the Chamizal Treaty, which was my crowning accomplishment in Mexico. In 1963, after my work on that treaty, I received a new posting in Washington. I was assigned to the Spanish Desk at the State Department, in part because I was bilingual and as a young man had studied in Spain and had dated girls in the Spanish embassy whose fathers now held important positions in the Spanish government. This was a critical juncture for U.S.-Spanish relations, as the U.S. was re-negotiating critically important treaties concerning its military base rights in Spain. We needed to secure the use of bases at Rota, Torrejón, Morón, and Zaragoza, and there was some potentially serious opposition in Spain. Our efforts to exercise a military presence in Spain formed a critical part of the U.S. policy of maintaining a massive deterrent to Soviet aggression. Along with nuclear-armed submarines and surface vessels, we sought to maintain nuclear-armed air patrols completely around the periphery of the Soviet Union in order to menace and contain the Soviets. Spain was critical to the success of this policy because it provided direct access to the southern regions of the Soviet Union, known as the "soft underbelly." For years, submarines out of Rota and airplanes loaded with nuclear bombs, patrolled back and forth constantly. Negotiating the treaties with Spain was very important business. I organized the signing ceremonies that capped our successful negotiations.

Franco—one of many dictators that I was to deal with in my career—was still in power when I began work on the Spanish Desk. One of my first initiatives in 1963 was to draft a message of condolence from the president to Señora Franco because everyone assumed that Franco could die at any time. Little did we know that he had another twelve years to go.

My new assignment gave me a whole new palette from which to paint. In my family life, we made some important changes also. As we were about to leave for Washington, my eldest son remarked, "Dad, how come we don't have a home like everybody else?" Knowing that it had been hard on my family to move every two or three years, that comment was like a dagger through my heart. While in Washington, we had always rented houses, but my son's comment fueled my resolve. I became determined that we would have our own home. We'd saved $2,000 in Mexico, and had recently inherited $3,000 from Dolores' grandfather. That gave us $5,000 for a down payment on a wonderful house in Chevy Chase that we purchased for $39,000.

My kids finally had a home they could call their own when we moved back to Washington. As new kids on the block, they had some adjustments to make. As we were unpacking, they went out to play with the neighborhood kids. In ten minutes, they came back crying, saying that the other kids didn't like them. "They won't play with us," they reported. "They say we're Italians." I said, "Well, tell them we're Spanish, not Italian." They went out and in a few minutes were back again, crying. "That's even worse!"

The house was cluttered with our half-unpacked belongings, but I took time to buy a gallon of black walnut ice cream and unpack bowls and spoons. When I called out to the children playing in the street that I had ice cream. They all came running. As we sat around the disheveled house, I explained to them that, even though my children spoke Spanish, we were Americans, just like them. That seemed to break the ice and pretty soon everyone was getting along. I advised my children not to speak Spanish around those kids, and that solved the problem, but soon they were speaking English all the time anyway.

There were problems of adjustment like that, as my children became familiar with American ways. They knew all about soccer, for example, but didn't have a clue about football. They'd watch a football game and say, "What are they doing?"

Soon after I began my job on the Spanish Desk, the assassination of President Kennedy plunged the entire country into deep grief. Nowhere was the grief and shock more profound than in Washington, where so many adored the Kennedy family. Anticipating that many world leaders would want to attend funeral services, the stunned State Department sent out a circular instruction to all U.S. Embassies flatly stating that the U.S. simply could not handle a flood of participants arriving from overseas. Foreign attendance at the funeral would be limited to foreign Ambassadors in Washington only.

No sooner had the circular instruction gone out than Embassy Madrid called to advise me that a high-level Spanish delegation headed by Vice-President and Captain General Augustín Muñoz Grandes was over the Atlantic en route to attend the Kennedy funeral. They added that the French Embassy in Madrid had called to confirm the precipitate Spanish action and to declare that since the Spanish were attending, de Gaulle would also.

So short was the notice that I just had time to rush to Andrews Air Base to receive the Spanish delegation. As he clumped down the plane's stairs, Muñoz Grandes headed straight for me, saying, "Frank, silly one, you should know you don't invite people to a funeral. They come."

Switching gears, the harried organizers of the intricate funeral preparations contacted me and State Department officers serving other geographic areas. They commissioned us to accompany the world leaders that, following Spain's example, were inundating Washington.

I will never forget those days as we hosted the world in a tribute to the fallen leader who had so much promise. I participated in the ceremonies, marches and meetings between world leaders and the bereaved family.

After the internment, we returned to the White House, where Jackie Kennedy planned to meet individually with the visiting dignitaries to express her gratitude and farewell. As I waited with the Spanish Vice-President for his turn to visit with Mrs. Kennedy, I became a witness to a curious but touching game involving Muñoz Grandes, Anastas Mikoyan, who represented the Soviet Union, and the Cardinal Secretary of State, representing the Pope.

Each of these worthies was determined that he should be the last to express condolences to Mrs. Kennedy. They held back as the dignitaries were escorted one at a time to the Red Room where Jackie waited. When only the three of them remained, none budged. Finally, the exasperated American Chief of Protocol said to the immobile luminaries, "Either you come now or Mrs. Kennedy will retire to her quarters without seeing you." After a pause Muñoz Grandes grumpily stepped forward. I witnessed a moving exchange between him and the composed widow and then with the President's mother. The Pope's representative succeeded in out-feinting the steely Russian to become the last to express sympathies.

I still have the funeral instructions among my papers. I read them and remember days that sorely tried our republic.

I had another sobering experience during my tenure on the Spanish Desk. A call at three in the morning on January 17, 1966 awakened me with the news that two American aircraft had collided over Spain and crashed. One of them was carrying four hydrogen bombs, one of which fell into the Mediterranean. All hell broke loose, as the Spanish and many others in the international community were in an uproar. Even though we eventually recovered all the warhead materials, including the one from the bottom of the ocean, the public remained terribly concerned that the area was polluted with radioactive material. Tourists began canceling their visits to Spain and people all over Europe boycotted Spanish fruits and vegetables for fear of contamination.

Struggling to defuse the situation, which grew in gravity during the long search for the missing bomb, I came up with an idea. I sent what would become a famous instruction to our Ambassador to Spain, Angier Biddle Duke. Everyone in Spain knew and liked Biddle Duke. He played well in the press, so I instructed him to proceed to Palmares on the coast to take a long swim in the Mediterranean. I also suggested that he eat many tomatoes in public, since Palmares was in the tomato producing region of Spain. Biddle Duke followed his instructions and, accompanied by his wife and two children and by a Spanish minister, cavorted publicly in the problem area. They were featured worldwide on newspaper front pages, freezing cold after swimming in the March sea but smiling as they ate tomatoes. That performance did a lot to quell the public's fear of contamination.[6]

The Spanish government wasn't as easy to appease, and we needed to maintain good relations for strategic defense reasons. So we agreed to remove several inches of topsoil from the entire crash site, put it in barrels, and ship it to South Carolina. Once we had promised to carry out that gargantuan task and assured Spain we would support her entry into international organizations, the Spanish got over their snit. Behind the scenes, though, the crash led to much more difficult complications. The accidental dropping of hydrogen warheads prompted the Spanish government to announce that they would no longer allow planes loaded with nuclear bombs to fly over Spain. The Moroccan government had already put such a prohibition in place just across from the Straits of Gibraltar from Spain. France also prohibited those flyovers.

Spain's decision to ban our nuclear-armed airplanes access to Spanish airspace meant that our cordon of bombers patrolling the Soviet underbelly could be broken, at a great cost to our national security. Fortunately, we worked out a solution that I think was brilliant. We called it "threading the needle." The Straits of Gibraltar, where the territorial waters of Spain and Morocco meet, are very narrow. We advised the Pentagon that if they directed the bombers smack down the middle of the straits, they would violate the airspace of neither

---

6. A 1967 book by Flora Lewis, "One of Our H-Bombs is Missing" gives a comprehensive account of the crisis.

Spain nor Morocco. If our planes would thread the needle at Gibraltar, they could continue on into the Mediterranean to resume their patrols. The plan was top secret at the time.

It was an unpublicized mystery as to how our planes continued their patrols, but a smart *New York Times* reporter, Benjamin Welles, eventually caught wind of the scheme. He came to me seeking confirmation, saying he was going to publish a story about our planes "threading the needle" at Gibraltar. I cautioned him that if he made our decision public, he would hurt U.S. interests. After a long talk, I persuaded him not to publish, and neither he nor anyone else ever did, as far as I know. The Departments of State and Defense learned that I had dissuaded Welles and congratulated me for it. Our defense treaty had been renewed. I count my role in the affair as a satisfying and significant accomplishment.

As my time on the Spanish Desk was drawing to a close, I, along with many others in the U.S. Government, worked hard to assure that Spain made a peaceful transition to democracy. I was proud to see that many of the initiatives I worked on were successful. U.S. loans and grants allowed Spain to develop an infrastructure that united all the regions of the country. Many of the young political and economic leaders whom we brought to the U.S. for training returned to Spain with new understanding of free markets and democratic political processes to help lead the country into a peaceful transition.

I ended my assignment in 1967 with high hopes for Spain's future and those hopes have been fulfilled. When the time for transition came in 1976–77, Spain gave the world an example of a remarkably peaceful change to a functioning democracy that still thrives to this day.

My performance on the Spanish Desk prompted my superiors to select me to attend the National War College at Fort Leslie McNair in Washington, where a limited number of the top officers of the State Department, CIA, Army, Navy, Air Force, and Coast Guard were sent for advanced training. We took intensive courses in national security, U.S. diplomatic and military history, negotiation, and other topics. It was assumed that graduates of the college would rise to the top of their various services. Almost all the State Department attendees became Ambassadors—the culmination of a career in the Foreign Service—and many of the military officers became heads of their respective services. They worked us hard at the War College, but for the first time in my career, I wasn't worked to near death. The college had plenty of sports facilities. I took up squash and took time for many other activities that I never had been able to do before. It was a wonderful experience not being tied down to a stressful job. I actually came to know and appreciate my family more fully.

At the end of the course, the College sent students to whichever part of the world they chose to visit. I elected to go to Latin America. During that tour, near the end of our stay in Guatemala, we visited Lake Atitlán, traveling overland from Chichicastenango. As we neared the lake, we began to descend a wildly curving road along a precipice that dropped off 200 or 300 feet to the lake. During the descent, as we talked about our trip, we noticed that the bus seemed to be going awfully fast—too fast for that curvy road. Then to my amazement, I saw one of our group, Doc Blanchard, rolling in the dust by the side of the road. He had jumped out of the bus, and soon two or three others followed. It dawned on me then that the brakes on the bus had failed. We were careening out of control. Fortunately, the driver didn't abandon his seat. Instead he tried to slow the bus by crashing it into the rocky bank on the uphill side of the road. He was having some success with this strategy, but I could see a very sharp curve coming up straight ahead and it seemed certain that we would fly off the road and over the precipice.

Just 20 yards before the curve, a front wheel came off the bus and we ground to a stop. We were all shaking as we exited the bus, thankful that the driver's quick thinking had saved our lives. We took up a collection to give him for his efforts and came to his defense when his boss threatened to fire him for damaging the bus. We never found out if the failed brakes were the result of sabotage, though some at the American Embassy suspected that was the case. In any event, that experience was one of several times that I had a very close brush with death.

We went on to visit several other countries during the War College tour. During our stay in Lima, Peru, I secured my next posting in the

Foreign Service. The Ambassador to Peru, Johnny Jones, asked to meet with me because, he said, he'd heard about me. He asked me to work for him as head of the political section. He added that it was a very good time to be in Peru. I accepted his offer enthusiastically.

We began moving out of our new home in Washington as I finished my course at the War College and prepared to leave for my new assignment. We packed our furniture and shipped it off to Lima. The last thing to go was the bed in Dolores' and my room. The kiddies slept on little mats on the floor for several days. When finally they came to take the matrimonial bed away, Dolores discovered that the headboard had left a mark on the wall. She insisted I repaint the wall before the renter—an officer from the Canadian Embassy—moved in. I protested that I had nothing to paint with, but she persisted, suggesting that I retrieve old clothes from the trash and buy paint and brushes from the hardware store.

Dolores and the kids went off to say goodbye to friends, leaving me alone in the house, getting more paint on myself than on the wall—when suddenly the doorbell rang. I looked out to see a great black limousine parked in front. I recognized it as the Spanish Ambassador's car. I went to the door in my tattered, paint-covered clothes to greet the chauffeur. We knew each other very well, but he was so embarrassed by my disheveled condition that he said, "Oh, I see Mr. Ortiz is not at home. When he returns, will you tell him that the Marqués de Merry del Val, the Ambassador of Spain, has sent him these farewell gifts? He and doña Mercedes wish Mr. and Mrs. Ortiz the best of fortune and good luck in their new assignment." I replied that I would be sure to give Mr. and Mrs. Ortiz the message.

The chauffeur returned to the car for the presents: case after case of fine wines, sherries, and cognacs—a touching testament to the friendship that we had built with the Spanish officials. I assured the driver that Mr. Ortiz would be very moved by this marvelous gift. He replied, "Well, tell Mr. Ortiz that the Ambassador wanted to be sure that he served these wonderful wines to remind him of Spain in his new post."

I surveyed the stack of cases, wondering what to do with them in the few hours I had before departing. I came up with a solution. I borrowed a shovel from a neighbor and struggled into the crawl space under the house and dug a large pit. By that time my kids had returned, and they handed me the bottles one by one until I had covered over the treasure of 100 or so bottles. By that time I was really filthy, but I got myself more or less clean and dressed and the family took off for Peru. We were gone for over six years. When we returned I could hardly wait to dig up the treasure. By then, all the labels had rotted off, so we had little clue what was in each bottle, but the wines and liqueurs had greatly improved with time. Who needs a wine cellar?

9

Peru: A Bizarre Accusation

Peru is one of the world's most varied, fascinating and challenging countries. Within its borders lie a section of the Andes, a mountain range that defies description; an arid coastal zone lined with lush, irrigated valleys; and a vast, nearly impenetrable rainforest in the Amazon drainage. The country's history is deeply layered. Lima, a great city still, held sway for nearly 300 years as a sophisticated vice-regal capital in the Spanish Empire. The beauty of its women is legendary.

I arrived in Lima in 1967 to assume my position as Political Officer at the U.S. Embassy. Lima in those days was a wondrous place. I came to know President Fernando Belaunde Terry very well. He was one of those people who is so good he's dangerous. I remember once taking a group of American senators to call on him. He showed us a relief map of a road he was building on the eastern, rainforest side of the Andes, a project he called the Marginal de la Selva. The senators were impressed because it was a huge proposition, and one asked, "Mr. President, do you have the money to build this?" Belaunde's reply took us all by surprise, "You know, the Incas didn't have money at all. They didn't even have a concept of money, and look what they accomplished. So I don't even think about money. I'm just going to do it." The senators looked at each other as if to say, "Who is this character?"

He was naïve, but a very good, constructive person, with all good intentions for his country. He was also a great admirer of the U.S., where he had been a university professor.

In 1968, there were rumblings around the capital that opposition elements were planning a military coup. This worried me because Belaunde was a great democrat, very honest, a visionary, and our friend. I learned that a group of those planning the coup often congregated at the Monterico racetrack in Lima. In order to get to know them I started spending time there. During one of my visits, two men pulled me aside. One of them, Enrique Leon Velarde, a demagogic mayor of San Martin de Porres, a very poor section of Lima, was very dangerous. The other, a Hollywood good-looking type, Pedro Garcia Miró, was the nephew of the owner of El Commercio, the most influential newspaper in Peru. These two informed me that they and others were determined to get rid of the "lunatic" president in a few days and wanted to know how the U.S. government would react. In strong terms I let them know that such an action would prompt a very negative response from the U.S., not only because it would be unconstitutional but because it would hurt Peru. "Once you start down that road," I warned them, "you'll have nothing but problems." I urged them to tell their military friends that it was a bad mistake to even think about it. They seemed to be listening.

The next morning, I reported my conversation to the Ambassador, who immediately called in the CIA Station Chief, the embassy's military attaché, and the number two officer in the embassy. He asked me to repeat my report and I told them I had heard that within days the army, with the backing of El Commercio, would stage a coup. I emphasized my belief that this was a credible threat and that we should report this to our government to consider the appropriate reaction. The Ambassador instructed the others in attendance to immediately check with their sources for verification, before he reported to Washington.

That afternoon the Ambassador called us all back to his office. The others reported that their contacts denied the threat of a coup. All three of these senior figures felt confident that the "rumor" as they called it, was absolutely untrue. The Ambassador turned to me and asked, "Frank, are you sure?" With confidence I replied, "Absolutely."

The Ambassador remained unsure about sounding the alarm to the State Department. I suggested he cover himself by sending a message that didn't commit him either way, simply stating that the head of the political section had heard credible rumors of an impending coup, and that the CIA and the military attachés checked with sources that summarily dismissed the threat. He sent the message with some misgivings, saying, "Won't sending such an ambiguous message seem odd?" My response was that we'd look worse if the coup happened and he hadn't reported our suspicions at all.

A few days later, on October 3, 1968 at two in the morning, while Dolores was in Panama and I was home with the four kids, I was awakened by a call from the head of the telephone company in Lima, an American with whom I had become friendly. He said, "I've got to be quick. The army is occupying my building. They're taking over the telephone exchanges and from my office I can see them battering down the iron gates to the presidential palace. There's a coup underway!" I thanked him and immediately called the Ambassador and told him the overthrow was in progress. He instructed me to wake up the CIA officer and the military attachés and for all of us to come to the embassy at once.

The Ambassador met me at the embassy, with the others straggling in a bit later. The rebels noticed that the embassy lights were going on and figured we were on to their actions. They immediately cut our electric lines, leaving us in the dark. I had to chuckle when I found out that the three men who had been so dismissive of me and so convinced that the coup was a fiction were trapped between floors in the elevator. It took us some time to get the embassy's generator going, but when it kicked in the lights came on and they were released.

It was a very difficult time at the embassy. When the dust had settled, however, the accuracy of my prediction raised my standing in the Service. The down side was that the coup changed the political climate in Peru entirely, replacing a government that was friendly to the U.S. with a hostile, leftist regime headed by General Juan Velasco Alvarado, a mestizo with a pronounced anti-American attitude. Fortunately, I was well acquainted with some top-ranking members of the new government. To protect American interests, I had to maintain my relationships with Leon Velarde and Garcia Miró, which was very hard for Dolores to endure. She considers those times the worst in our career because she detested those people and their politics. They were corrupt and insensitive—not nice people by any stretch.

Leon Velarde often would invite government officials and a crowd of Mafia types on excursions on his big yacht, the Mariah. Dolores and I were often included. Dolores hated every minute of it, but it was very useful for me, because it gave me close access to the inner circles of the government. Schmoozing with the junta and their pals allowed me to keep abreast of their activities and to look after American interests, which were my primary responsibility.

Not long after the coup, the new government began expropriating American businesses. They started with International Petroleum Company and much later moved on to Chuck Robinson's iron ore company and other businesses until they gradually took over most American interests in Peru, including the telephone company. The U.S., while acknowledging the government's sovereign right to expropriate businesses, protested and sought compensation for the American owners. That went on for some time and I was sometimes caught in the middle of difficult situations.

Through it all I maintained good relationships with my contacts in the ruling regime. This assured that I had access to them, but it led to some problems for me. I began to notice the Communist press, which supported the government, repeatedly zeroing in on me, claiming I was the head of the CIA in Latin America masquerading as a diplomat. Peruvian groups were fomenting the rumors, but the KGB was probably behind them. They painted me as a very dangerous type. I informed the Ambassador that the leftists were out to get me. We agreed that I had to be very careful, though we were confident that they wouldn't try to kill me. They did, however, try all sorts of ways to get to me. All this made life stressful for me, but I kept up with my responsibilities.

One evening the Ambassador—a new one, Toby Belcher—called me at home and asked me to come to the embassy immediately. The number two man and the CIA Station Chief were waiting with him when I arrived. Ambassador Belcher proceeded to tell me that he had just been summoned by the Peruvian Foreign Minister, who had advised him that the Peruvian government had uncovered a plot to assassinate President Velasco Alvarado. The worst part of this astonishing claim was that the minister said I was behind the scheme. He charged that I intended to have the president killed from an overpass on the speedway. The Foreign Minister formally demanded that I leave the country within 72 hours. He further implicated the labor attaché, John Dougherty, and the station chief of the CIA in the plot and demanded that they also leave. His tour having ended, Dougherty had left months before. That left me, the most public figure of those accused, to confront these incredible charges.

I reminded the Ambassador that he and everyone else knew that the charge was a wild fabrication. He assured me he had the utmost confidence in me and that he and the whole embassy knew it wasn't true. However, the number two man at the embassy was less than supportive. He said, "Frank, I think you'd better be packing." I was vehemently opposed to such a course, arguing that by departing I would, in effect, give credence to a great falsehood. I flatly refused to go. The number two man's response was—and I never forgave him for it, even though he's a good friend—"Frank, think of the interests of our country. If you refuse to go, it will undo all the good things you've done here." My retort was that giving in would amount to an admission that I was part of an assassination plot. That was a very serious admission that would permanently damage my reputation as a diplomat. Worst of all, I was in a very difficult position, because I couldn't prove a negative. How could I prove that I wasn't involved in a plot that didn't exist?

The Ambassador, reluctant to make a decision on this major problem, reported to the State Department in Washington and waited for instructions. I was very pleased when a stinging reply came back, ordering the Ambassador to demand an urgent meeting with the foreign minister. He was to tell the minister that the charges he made against three American officers were the most serious charges ever leveled against American diplomats in the history of U.S. relations with Peru. He was to inform the minister that he could not make such charges without substantiation and to demand that the minister provide evidence establishing my role in the alleged assassination plot.

Belcher carried out these instructions with the foreign minister, General Mercado Jarrín, who responded, predictably, that giving proof would compromise intelligence sources. The Ambassador replied as instructed by Washington that if Mercado could not provide some basis for these very serious charges, the U.S. would reject them out of hand. Furthermore, if the regime insisted that I leave, the U.S. would expel from Washington the Ambassador of Peru and four other diplomats.

I was delighted that the State Department stood behind me. The Peruvians didn't respond to the Ambassador's demands. They provided no evidence of even the existence of a plot. The whole silly affair was hushed up and I remained at my post for eight more months, until my normal tenure ended. This experience was the most bizarre in my career. It gave me an inkling of what it meant to be in bad graces with the Soviet KGB.

Near the end of our stay in Peru, I had another one of those experiences that drove home for me the fickleness of fate. Dolores and I and another couple, Teddy Blaque and his wife Dorey, had plans to leave Peru about the same time for new assignments. The Ambassador suggested that we all take a trip together before leaving. He and his wife would accompany us. He proposed that I arrange a trip to the Huaylas Valley, a Shangri-La-like place high in a valley between the Black and White mountain ranges. The valley, renowned for its fertility and its lovely towns and people, was extremely isolated. The only practical way to get there in those days was to take a narrow-track railway, placing your automobile on a flat bed railcar.

Yungay, a town in the valley, was the hometown of Bishop Bambaren of Lima, who sent word ahead to his relatives that we would be coming and they should take good care of us. I put a lot of work into making reservations at the hotel and for the train for the last weekend of May, 1970—Memorial Day weekend. About two weeks before our planned departure, Dorey asked me to change the dates to one week earlier, since she and Teddy were packed to leave and were quite uncomfortable where they were staying. I protested that I'd put in too much effort already, that people had been notified, reservations made, etc., going so far as to tell her that if she and Teddy couldn't come on the planned weekend, we'd invite someone else.

Dorey went to the Ambassador and told him I was being beastly. He called me in and forcefully suggested I change the schedule to accommodate the Blaques. So grumblingly, I did.

On the Sunday of our excursion in Huaylas, we left our hotel to drive up to a beautiful lake at the base of Huascaran, at 22,200 feet the highest mountain in Peru. The magnificent peak glistened with snow and glaciers and the lake was like heaven. Teddy fished and we had a picnic lunch. The Ambassador napped while Dolores and I took a long walk down the road. It was an idyllic day. Our party left at five in the afternoon, as it became quite cold. We drove from the lake to the town of Yungay below, a beautiful little colonial town with a plaza and a church. Bishop Bambaren's family had expected us a week later, but I knocked on the door and reminded them that the Bishop had asked that we visit them. Bambaren's two sisters and mother requested that we give them a half hour to get ready. We walked around the lovely town, surprised to see palm trees at that high altitude, and then we went back to the house, a substantial old colonial building with thick stone walls and stone floors. It was freezing inside, but the dining room table was littered with sardines and cookies and a cake, and on and on. Our hosts made us tea and then one of them began playing the piano and the other the guitar and they said, "Let's dance!" We danced and had a great time.

Later in Huaraz we dined with the local Peace Corps volunteers. I met a plain-looking young girl from New Jersey named Caroline, a fine young Irish American guy, and a couple of others. We brought them treats and Dolores made them corn bread in a big tin over an open fire. There was music and Caroline told me that living in Huaylas was the happiest time in her life. She confided in me a great deal, telling me of the indifference of her family in New Jersey and how she felt ignored in the U.S. "People need me and love me here. I'm so happy here," she said. I asked for her parents' names and promised her to tell them we had seen her. She was thrilled and asked me to mention how well she was doing, because they thought little of the Peace Corps and didn't support her going to Peru. I assured her I'd tell them what a great job she was doing.

We made the trip back to Lima and everybody was happy. The Ambassador thanked me for making such perfect arrangements and said he'd never forget that trip. Then, one week after we returned, tragedy struck: at three on a Sunday afternoon—just the time we would have been at the lake by the mountain—there was a tremendous earthquake in the Andes. A huge block of ice from Huascaran peak fell into the lake, sending a wall of water rushing down the valley that completely destroyed Yungay. The earthquake killed 60,000 people, including all of the Bambaren family.

We missed sudden death by a week, all because Dorey Blaque insisted on that change in plans. I chalk it up to good luck that saved us from being up there. We could never have survived. The experience was one of life's basic lessons: death is always a factor in life.

Later, when relief services were getting underway, First Lady Pat Nixon came down from Washington with a planeload of emergency supplies and clothing for the victims. Dolores became very involved in the effort as planes dropped supplies into the affected villages. The wives of officers in the military government came to help, too, but Dolores noticed that they took the best things from the relief supplies for themselves. They'd display an article of clothing and say, "This is perfectly good! You don't want to drop it to those dirty Indians."

Our new friend Caroline was killed in the quake. Unfortunately, she did what you shouldn't do in an earthquake: she ran out into a narrow street, and the buildings collapsed on her. I felt it my duty to call her parents with the sad news. Much to my surprise, their response, without any indication of grief, was, "How much is it going to cost us to bring her back? Will the government pay for it—do we have to pay for it?" Remembering their daughter's comments, I made a suggestion.

"You know," I said, "I think that Caroline would prefer to be buried here in Peru. She loved it here. She had a lot of good friends who really cared for her." They asked if I was kidding and I assured them that it was true. I offered to see that she received a decent burial at a good gravesite. They assented, providing that they didn't have to pay for anything. So Caroline is buried in Huaraz.

Our last night in Lima President Velasco Alvarado invited us to a dinner for Mrs. Nixon—the same Velasco Alvarado that I had been accused of trying to murder. During dinner, the Minister of Interior, General Artola, took me aside to say, "Frank, I hope you understand that it was for political reasons that we were trying to get rid of you." I told him that I knew that. He offered his apology to me, and I accepted it. But when I inquired if he was speaking on behalf of the government, he said that no, he was apologizing just for himself. He explained that he didn't have a very big role in the affair but that he was sorry nevertheless and he wished me well in my next tour of duty. I made sure to let him know how difficult it had made my life in Peru. He shrugged it off, saying, "Well, that sort of thing happens in politics." President Velasco Alvarado was very cold to me at the dinner. He made no effort to apologize.

Many years later General Mercado Jarrín revealed the political machinations behind the effort to expel me from Peru. The story was written up and published in more than one place in Peru and other Latin American countries, and much later in the U.S. Mercado Jarrín wrote that he had tried to stop the military leaders from persecuting me, but that others in the regime wanted badly to get me out of the country. They thought I was too close to the leadership and knew them from the inside too well. They were right. I understood the way they operated and cautioned others closely to evaluate everything they said. For example, when our government sent an upstanding man, Under Secretary of State Jack Irwin, to arrange compensation for confiscated U.S. properties, Peruvian officials tried to pull the wool over his eyes by making promises they had no intention of keeping. I warned Irwin not to believe their ruse and to press harder. This was not convenient for the military government.

In spite of the efforts of the military regime and their KGB-inspired cohorts to discredit me, my legacy in Lima remains very positive. My reputation in the Foreign Service also was untarnished as we left Peru en route to my next, much more difficult assignment, Montevideo, Uruguay.

10

Uruguay: Living with Terror

My posting in Montevideo, Uruguay in 1970 was a really rough experience. Uruguay is one of the most admirable countries in the world, with some of the most educated and ethical people I know. Uruguay effected comprehensive state welfare programs in the nineteen-teens, just shortly after Sweden established a groundbreaking system of general social welfare. Uruguay also is one of the most democratic countries in the world, with a very high literacy rate and average level of education. In Uruguay you could go from kindergarten to a Ph.D. free of cost. Medical services were very good and very cheap. A new mother was given a couple of years off of work to take care of her newborn. One could be eligible for retirement at a young age. Music, art, and a creative cultural life flourished.

My family and I would have been extremely happy in Uruguay, except for the fact that about four years before we arrived, the economic system collapsed. The price of wool and meat dropped precipitously, causing the welfare state to buckle. There was no money to run the hospitals. The universities, although also broke, continued turning out thousands of professionals each year, even though there was almost no demand for them. Young engineers were out of work, new doctors driving taxis. This was fertile ground for a populist reaction. A Marxist group called the Tupamaros, who despised everything American, began violent terrorist activities against the existing democratic power structure.

The Tupamaros were the most cunning, most dangerous terrorist group that I had encountered. They employed a truly effective strategy: every Friday they would strike, killing or kidnapping, blowing up power lines—all manner of destructive attacks. Throughout the week, everyone would absorb the previous week's damage and wonder what the Tupamaros would do the next Friday.

Our immersion into this chaotic and violent situation was immediate. My first duty, on my first day in Montevideo, was to attend a memorial service for Dan Mitrioni, a former state chief of police from New Mexico who headed a U.S. mission to train the Uruguayan police to combat terrorism. Just four days before we arrived, the Tupamaros had kidnapped Mitrioni during a carefully organized operation against American Embassy officials. They also captured the head of the commercial section of the embassy by hitting him on the head, wrapping him in a rug, and tying him down in the back of a pickup. Fortunately, he worked his ties loose and jumped out of the pickup while it was speeding down the road. The terrorists also tried to take the cultural attaché. They jumped him in the garage of his apartment building, but he honked his car horn, attracting attention and scaring off his would-be captors. But poor Mitrioni—they tied him up, tortured him, and finally killed him.

Such was the state of affairs when I arrived to assume my job as Deputy Chief of Mission, the number two position in the embassy. I knew that things were terribly bad in Uruguay, but wasn't at all prepared for the situation on the ground. "Why doesn't the Department give me a nice, peaceful post?" I wondered. The State Department's rationale was that I had the skills and abilities required to protect American interests in Uruguay. The unspoken reason, though, was that nobody wanted to be assigned there and I hadn't refused the assignment—an action I would never consider taking.

We endured three years of constant, extreme tension in Montevideo. As Deputy Chief, I was assigned a very nice house with a swimming pool, but we couldn't go outside and enjoy the grounds because of fear of snipers or kidnappers. For security, the embassy soon moved us into an apartment on the fourth floor near downtown. The apartment house was surrounded by open parks, which made it easier to watch for suspicious activity. We felt threatened nonetheless, and once a nearby bomb explosion knocked us out of bed.

We sent our children out of the country, except for the littlest one, and Dolores made sure she was seldom photographed so the terrorists couldn't identify her and make her a target. She took buses to get around to avoid being associated with an embassy car.

A couple of years into my posting, Ambassador Adair and his wife decided to take home leave. They had long suffered under terrible pressure. As prime terrorist targets, both the Ambassador and I needed constant personal protection by bodyguards. We always traveled in separate, armored sedans, his accompanied by two other protective vehicles. Adding to the Ambassador's anxiety, the Tupamaros had recently kidnapped the Ambassador of Great Britain, Geoffrey Jackson, and held him for eight months. Jackson's capture was a consequence of his failure to observe the first rule of survival in these conditions: never follow a predictable routine. He went to the office at the same time every day, by the same route. He knew full well this was foolish behavior, and told me he feared something would eventually happen to him. Fortunately, Jackson survived his captivity and wrote a book about his experience, *Surviving the Long Night.*

I took over the embassy when the Ambassador and his wife departed. He wished me well with an assurance that I would do fine, since by then I had "become accustomed to the pressure." I didn't feel so comfortable as our exposure to terrorist action was now even greater. We moved into the Ambassador's residence, which was surrounded by pillboxes sheltering armed guards and other protection.

The Ambassador thought his troubles were over when he and his wife boarded the plane to leave Uruguay, but on the second leg of their flight home, from Santiago, Chile to Miami, a bomb exploded in the baggage hold as they flew over the Caribbean. Fortunately, the blast didn't destroy the plane. It made a forced landing, but this was the last straw for them. They decided they couldn't take anymore and announced they were retiring from the Service—a decision that left me holding the bag in Uruguay. Although I was promised that a new Ambassador would be arriving soon, nobody wanted the post, leaving me to serve as *Chargé d'Affaires* in the Montevideo embassy for a year.

With the Ambassador's departure I assumed not only his responsibilities; I also filled his profile as a prime target for the terrorists. We were somewhat accustomed to the anxiety by then. We already had our kids in school out of the country and felt relatively secure in the embassy residence. However, the situation in Uruguay continued to deteriorate. Ironically, the democratic traditions of the country worked against its security when it came to fighting terrorism. Although faced with the terrorist crisis, the army, out of respect for democratic traditions, spurned domestic law enforcement and stayed out of the picture. The terrorists, for their part, were careful not to mess with the army, so the responsibility for fighting terrorist activities fell to the civilian police, who simply were not equipped to cope with such a formidable adversary as the Tupamaros, equipped as they were with automatic weapons while the police had only revolvers.

I shall always remember one of the worst of those dark days. It was early in 1973, on a Friday. At six o'clock, the Tupamaros assassinated the chief of naval intelligence. At seven, they gunned down the deputy chief of police on his way to work. The streetcar power station blew up at eight o'clock, and at nine there was an attempt to kidnap the vice-minister of education. At ten o'clock the terrorists blew up a power pylon. By this time, the city was in panic, made worse by the fact that the news media were not allowed to report in depth on the Tupamaros or their activities. News spread through exaggerated and inaccurate rumors.

That morning, the president called a joint session of congress and asked for a declaration of a state of internal war, which would allow him to order the army to fight the terrorists. The congress didn't need much persuading and their declaration of internal war unleashed the army, which promptly began rounding up terrorists, killing some of them. The military resorted to some extreme measures. President

Bordaberry, with whom I was close, tried to rein them in, insisting on fair trials for the accused terrorists. But the armed forces persisted with their heavy-handed response to the terrorists and demanded military control of the government.

Some military and political leaders contacted me to inform me of their intention to ask the president to step down. I discouraged them and reminded them that their constitution did not empower them to do that. I added that the consequences would be very harmful. I contacted the State Department and the Brazilian and Argentine Ambassadors, who were influential and also were very much concerned about the turn of events. We resolved to make a joint effort to head off a military coup, but we were not successful. I found myself in the middle of another coup. It was hard to believe it was happening in Uruguay, of all places.

Fortunately, the military crackdown did make Uruguay a safer place, and the junta returned control to a civilian government fairly quickly. The State Department named a new Ambassador—with the terrorists under control it was easier to find recruits—which meant I could leave.

Dealing with the terrorist threat dominated much of our lives in Uruguay, but we worked on many projects besides. Our embassy did much good to bring about the country's economic recovery. For example, we helped the Uruguayans put their wonderful wools to good use in making clothes for the American market. Some industries we helped develop were so good, in fact, that their excellence overwhelmed them. I once recommended to Sears Roebuck that they consider buying leather jackets from Uruguay. Thrilled at the business prospects, the manufacturer sent off samples, which led to huge orders—10,000 leather jackets at a time! The manufacturer called me and said, "Frank, you've ruined me. These people need 10,000 leather jackets within three weeks and I can't possibly do that!" In general, though, we helped many Uruguayans realize the tremendous export potential of their products, which led to an improvement in the economic situation.

In spite of the difficulties, we have fond memories of our time in Uruguay. We had an opportunity to return 24 years later, in 1997, while our son Jamie was working there. We found old friends whose warm welcome reminded us of the good times we had enjoyed there. In 1973, however, at the time of our departure, we were glad to leave and looked forward to an assignment that would take us back to our home in Washington.

11

Back to the Home Office: The Southern Cone and Working with Kissinger

In 1973, after our Montevideo posting, I was assigned to Washington to be in charge of the Southern Cone—the countries of Uruguay, Paraguay, and Argentina. Chile, although geographically part of the "cone," presented a unique situation, so it was dealt with separately. I was only in that office for about a year, but it was a very eventful year.

Early on during my time working on the Southern Cone, I concluded that the person in Argentina most able to help reduce the anti-U.S. feelings there was Juan Domingo Perón. After living in exile for 18 years, Perón had only recently returned to Argentina and won back the presidency at a critical time for his country.

Argentina's very fine Ambassador to the U.S., Alejandro Orfila, worked with me to arrange a meeting between Presidents Nixon and Perón. We believed they could get along and perhaps solve some of the endemic problems in the relationship between the two countries. We knew full well that Perón would never visit Washington because it would give the impression that he was coming hat-in-hand, seeking financial help. At the same time, Nixon would never go to Buenos Aires because of the anti-Americanism there. So we thought of a good idea: Perón would come to New York and address the United Nations General Assembly, which is like addressing the world and would certainly appeal to him. On his way back, he would stop at Camp David to meet with Nixon. The White House liked the idea and the plans were set.

I was very enthusiastic about the planned meeting—then Perón decided to die. All our beautiful plans collapsed, but in developing them I had gotten to know many of the top people in Argentina, and I got along with them fine. For example, the State Department invited one of Argentina's great leaders, Senator Italo Luder for a visit. I escorted him around, and we got along extremely well. I arranged for him to be presented on the floor of the U.S. Senate, which moved him greatly.

As part of the U.S. delegation chosen to attend Perón's funeral, I was amazed at the hundreds of thousands of people standing in line waiting to view his casket. I could no longer doubt he was a political leader much loved by the Argentine majority. He did awful things and caused terrible, lasting damage to Argentina but there was no question he was beloved, especially among the working classes. Many worried about what lay ahead for Argentina.

I was working on Argentine issues when President Nixon resigned. It's a day I will never forget. I was at dinner in the Argentine embassy. The guests, myself included, were thunderstruck by the news. I had seldom experienced the oppressive climate of crisis and uncertainty that then gripped Washington as Gerald Ford assumed the presidency. Many were not sure what lay ahead for the U.S. Ford's appointment of Henry Kissinger as Secretary of State was reassuring.

Ford was easier to work for, but the presidency clearly wore on him and his wife. The Fords began their term being wonderful, down home, easy-to-approach people. Soon after he took over the presidency, though, they both began to withdraw. They began to avoid eye contact because meeting someone's glance would inevitably lead to an in-your-face hounding. Too many wanted something from them. Dolores and I noted the change and commented on how sad it was that Ford and his wife could not behave as normal people anymore.

The Nixon resignation was a major distraction, but I soon resumed my work with Argentina. Perón's third wife, Maria Isabel (Isabelita), succeeded him as President of Argentina. I was amused when the

Argentine press criticized me for referring to the new president as "*la Presidenta.*" They wrote that the proper term, even for a woman, was "*el Presidente.*" The Royal Academy of the Spanish Language in Madrid came to my defense; she remained "la Presidenta" and some Argentines saw me as a skilled linguist—a hilarious notion to a New Mexican.

Maria Isabel was a real bimbo. Perón's previous wife, Evita, had been a tremendous asset to him politically, but Isabel lacked Evita's finesse. Maria Isabel, who came from a questionable background, allowed shady characters to run the government for her. When Perón met Maria Isabel, she was a dancer in a Panamanian nightclub that I had visited with some classmates during my National War College tour. Our group had gone to the club because of its reputation as a venue for good music. A pretty girl sat next to me and tried to entice me by saying, "I'm a natural blonde, see?" and she held her armpit up to my face for proof. Such were the haunts of Isabelita before she became Argentina's First Lady and then President of Argentina.

Not surprisingly, Isabelita's presidency rapidly became a disaster. It was under her leadership—or lack thereof—that Argentina's terrible "dirty war" began. Needless to say, I did not look forward to being responsible for relations with Isabelita's Argentina, but once more my luck held, as fate's finger soon nudged me elsewhere.

In the midst of my involvement with Argentina and the Southern Cone, Secretary of State Henry Kissinger agreed for me to work in his office as one of two Deputy Executive Secretaries of State. The two of us, along with Kissinger's executive secretary, funneled official papers and reports to and from Kissinger. I'd worked before with the Undersecretary of State, but this was my first direct assignment with the Secretary himself. We served as liaisons between the State Department and other departments; my particular connections were with the White House and the Pentagon. My contacts put me in communication with senior staff in both those executive departments.

Kissinger was demanding, unfriendly and, I thought, extremely insecure. He would bring his big dog Tyler to the office and have the junior officers take the loveable beast out for walks. When work was taken to him, typically he'd say, "Is this the best you can do?" His rough management style wore on us all. Fortunately, others in the office compensated for his abrasive manner. Working with the Deputy Secretary of State, Chuck Robinson, who was a close friend since my time in Peru (and who lives in Santa Fe) was especially rewarding.

One of my responsibilities was to manage the Operations Center, an office on the same floor as that of the Secretary of State. We were equipped with the most modern communications. In an instant we could reach the American embassy in Beijing or the American consulate in Puerto de la Cruz, or whomever we wanted. All the most important, most sensitive cables from the field came through my office.

My position in the Secretary's office brought huge responsibilities, placing me under very high pressure. This had an effect on my family and me. I would often go to work at 7:30 in the morning and get home at 9:30 at night. Those were tough years, not only because of the working hours but, in large measure, because of the difficulty of working for Kissinger. It was astounding how demanding he could be. I'd get calls saying, "The Secretary wanted such and such—why the hell didn't you get it to him?" I was required to subordinate myself totally to the Secretary's needs. He seemed quite insensitive and never encouraging to those of us who served him.

Having succeeded in extracting us from the disaster in Southeast Asia and engineering an opening to Communist China, Henry Kissinger had already achieved great and laudable successes. His next focus was to resolve the Israeli-Palestinian conflict, a seemingly intractable problem that he tackled full-steam. Kissinger believed in direct negotiation, which meant he traveled often to the Middle East, a procedure the press called "shuttle diplomacy." From the NODIS (No Distribution) reporting telegrams he sent back from the Middle East, it was clear he had been successful in establishing excellent relationships with regional leaders, particularly in Egypt and Jordan. Unfortunately, the intensity of the conflict between the Israelis and the Palestinians was too great for even a master negotiator like Kissinger. The Democrats' victory in 1976 put a final end to Kissinger's efforts and he returned to private life.

I hated to see Kissinger go, for in spite of my personal difficulties in meeting his demands, I had a deep admiration for him. I later formed a good personal relationship with him. I believe he was one of the best secretaries of state we have ever had. Unlike all the others I worked for, Kissinger was thinking ten, twenty—even fifty years ahead. Others tended to focus on how a particular decision would play in the next day's *New York Times,* or how it would affect the fall elections. Kissinger kept the big picture in mind. I greatly admired him for that.

I think Kissinger sensed my admiration. When I went in to say goodbye to him on his last day as Secretary of State, his eyes welled up with tears. He later came to visit us in Peru and Argentina. I took him to Machu Picchu and made him climb up and down steep trails. As he was huffing and puffing, I'd say, "Henry, is that the best you can do?" reminding him of his oft-repeated line in Washington. He wasn't sure what to do with that sarcastic comment.

My years in Kissinger's office were eventful and rewarding. I was at the epicenter of the State Department's business. I was in charge of the distribution of NODIS cable traffic—messages, including many personal ones, that were so sensitive that only a few designated people were allowed to see them. Handling this traffic made me aware of many sensitive actions that were going on during those tumultuous years. Not all of these exchanges were earth-shaking serious. I enjoyed exchanges between Kissinger in the field and Larry Eagleburger, his all-purpose man in the State Department. Captioned "odds and ends," those cables made delicious reading.

The next election, in 1976, put Jimmy Carter in power. He named Cyrus Vance Secretary of State and Warren Christopher Deputy Secretary of State. Kissinger and Chuck Robinson left the State Department, but Vance and Christopher kept me on to help smooth the transition. It was a good idea but unfortunately it didn't work out so well. I had been in the State Department's front office for over two years and had my own ideas about how things should be run. Perhaps I knew too much, and often my ideas differed from those of the new staff. It became clear to me that it was probably a good time for me to return to the field. President Carter, with a little nudging from the State Department, gave me my first ambassadorial posting—and it was to a destination where I never dreamed I'd serve.

12

Barbados and the Caribbean: Reaching the Top Rungs of the Ladder

Dolores and I shall always remember our stay in the Caribbean, my first ambassadorship, for the wonderful people there, who were so kind to us. They made us feel we were a part of their remarkable communities. My embassy was in Bridgetown, Barbados, but my posting was Ambassador to Barbados and Grenada, and special representative to Antigua, St. Kitts-Nevis, Anguilla, Dominica, St. Lucia, and St. Vincent. Each one of these beautiful little tropical islands had a prime minister brimming with self-importance. Each individual was markedly different in terms of personality, but most were very demanding. My experience in dealing with these diverse leaders, gave me a crash course in acting.

Diplomacy to some degree *is* acting. As a diplomat, you can never be completely frank about your opinions. You dissimulate them. If someone asks what you think of an idea, you can't simply say, "It stinks," even if that's what you think. As Dolores taught me, you must say, "That's very interesting." You can loathe somebody, but if he or she has the power to affect important U.S. interests, you must try to get along. Making an effort to be agreeable preserves one's capacity to influence political leaders and governments' policies. A diplomat must not have a proprietary attachment to his ideas. A diplomat succeeds when he convinces the person across the table to almost unwittingly lay claim to and adopt the diplomat's ideas as his own.

So often at the end of a day you're dog-tired and want to enjoy a quiet evening at home, but it's the French National Day or the Canadian Ambassador's farewell, or whatever. If you don't attend the event it could be a major problem, a diplomatic snub, so you attend and try to radiate interest and charm. You hate to drink warm blood, which I've had to do, or eat things that you find unpalatable or disgusting. But you say, "This is wonderful," and you do it.

The only place I drew the line on accepting drinkable offerings was in the highlands of Peru. There, the Indians drink *chicha,* an alcoholic drink made by chewing corn kernels and spitting the masticated mass into a pot with a narrow opening. The ladies sit all day chewing and spitting into the *olla,* which they then cover and let ferment. When the poor, hapless American Ambassador—that's me—arrives, they say, "We've made the most wonderful chicha just for you." And a dear lady ladles some into a dirty cup. When this happened, I drew the line. I pressed my lips to the cup, took a small drop, and said, "Wonderful!" Then I put the cup down and was sure to surreptitiously spill it out of sight on the dirt floor.

My relaxed time in the Caribbean spared me many of these diplomatic horrors, but I did have to learn to deal with some strange individuals. Because each island's prime minister had a distinct personality, I had to tailor my approach on each island. Some prime ministers were difficult and quite pompous. On St. Lucia, the prime minister was a fine upstanding person. He was intelligent and very quiet, and we worked well together. I felt very comfortable with him. In Dominica, the prime minister was a dynamic, wonderful woman. I won her over by being especially courteous, opening doors, and calling her "ma'am."

Grenada was a different story. The Prime Minister, Sir Eric Gairy, was strange. He was basically mad. He believed he talked to God, that he had encountered a flying saucer, and that he had spoken with little green men. When I presented credentials, he insisted that all the unfortunate people in attendance at the ceremony go to a bar he owned called the Gold Room. He kept ordering champagne, expecting me to pay for it. We were being eaten alive by mosquitoes. It was a terrible night.

After a short while in Grenada, I grew tired of Sir Eric's frequent pleas for money. To help him out, I suggested that Grenada issue a series of postage stamps featuring UFOs. He did so and the impoverished state made lots of money as stamp collectors worldwide snapped up this unusual issue. Sir Eric beamingly told me I was an "all right guy." (I blush as I make this confession.)

In spite of the difficulty of working with Gairy, my time as Ambassador in the Caribbean was great, especially after our experience in Uruguay, where enemies conspired to kill me. In Barbados, I enjoyed driving my own official car, even though I had a chauffeur at my disposal. I had no need for bodyguards and was free to go anyplace on the islands. Dolores and I attended many local festivals on the small islands, so many people came to know us personally. For me, this was a big relief after almost a decade of terrible stress, during which, among other things, I was accused of being an assassin, stalked by would-be assassins, used by the CIA, and under constant pressure abroad and in Washington. In Barbados, I'd often just lie for hours on the beach. That was quite a change.

Barbados, where the British Royal family often vacations, is more British than England. We came to know Princess Margaret, a very troubled person who seemed to enjoy telling me dirty jokes. Once, three former British prime ministers came to a party at our house. When Dolores sent a photo from that party to her cousin in Great Britain, her cousin commented that it would be impossible to entertain three prime ministers together in London. But in Barbados it was easy. You'd almost fall over them on the beach. The island was also popular with movie stars and other celebrities. We had a great life and we relished our two years there.

With only five resident Ambassadors in Barbados, the diplomatic circles were much smaller than those we'd experienced elsewhere. In addition to U.S. Ambassador, I bore the high-sounding title of Dean of the Diplomatic Corps of Barbados. In that role, I played a ceremonial part in the visit of the Queen of England to the islands. The

Queen, well advised to bring diamond-studded tiaras and other showy jewels with her, sparkled and glowed like a sun goddess. Even the most jaded were overwhelmed by her radiating brilliance.

During my time in the Caribbean, President Carter courageously and against much opposition, returned the Panama Canal Zone to Panamanian control. I believe he was right in that decision. To celebrate the signing of the treaty, American Ambassadors in the Western Hemisphere received instructions to accompany our chiefs of state to Washington, where the signing ceremony was to be held. The plan was for each head of state to have one-on-one time with the president.

Many Caribbean prime ministers decided not to attend, but the strange one, Sir Eric Gairy, decided to go. I promised the White House I would make Sir Eric's time with President Carter very brief—only 10 minutes. I intended to move Sir Eric in and out before he could say or do something ridiculous. The White House staff agreed because they preferred to spare the president an uncomfortable experience.

As it neared the appointed hour when Sir Eric was to call on the president, I went to pick him up at his suite in a hotel. As I entered his suite, I noticed in the foyer a large box wrapped in purple crepe paper and a big pink bow. I wondered what it could possibly be.

Sir Eric's valet greeted me saying that Sir Eric was so nervous, he couldn't tie his tie and he wouldn't allow his valet to do it. He asked if I would help him. I said of course and tied it. Sir Eric cut an impressive figure in his London suit. He asked me if he looked all right and I assured him that he looked fine but reminded him we couldn't be late and had to leave. We rode to the White House in a great limousine flying the Grenadian and American flags and accompanied by motorcycle policemen.

The President was meeting the foreign leaders in the room next to the Oval Office. President Carter was sitting at the head of a large table. Sir Eric entered and sat to the President's left with me beside him. Zbigniew Brzezinski, the National Security Advisor, was seated opposite to us. The President and Sir Eric exchanged niceties. My job was to write an official memorandum of what I expected would be a very brief conversation.

"I'm glad you came," said the President, "this is a very important action by the United States." Sir Eric congratulated him for this, saying, "You bring peace. We all love you." Then Sir Eric took things where I'd feared he would. He told the president that before he came he had talked to God, who told him what he should say. I thought, "I've got to put this in the memo." I was embarrassed and wondered how Carter would reply.

To my surprise, Carter, a kind, gentle person, didn't miss a beat. He said he did not talk to God, that he was not that privileged. He explained that while he was not good enough for God to favor, his sister Ruth did have that privilege. "Ruth tells me what God says," he said. Well, lo and behold, this got the conversation going and the two of them started to gel. Sir Eric asked about God's modalities when he talked to Carter's sister. Did God's voice come from up above and the right, or from low to left? he wanted to know. The President said he'd never thought to ask but would inquire. Carter told Sir Eric that he firmly believed that he received divine inspiration through his sister Ruth. Sir Eric was glowing. As far as I could tell, Carter was being sincere.

The conversation continued, becoming more unusual every minute. Sir Eric reported that he had seen a flying saucer and talked with the beings inside it. "They're not bad people," he commented. Carter replied that he, too, had seen a flying saucer, and that everybody knew it since he said so publicly. The President described his sighting, which took place as he was driving in Georgia. The saucer didn't land, he saw no aliens, but the President had definitely seen a UFO. They continued to talk about flying saucers, both enjoying every minute.

The conversation went on and on. I couldn't believe my ears. The two of them were getting along famously. Twenty minutes went by, then thirty, and finally the U.S. Chief of Protocol, my friend Abelardo Valdez, came in and gave me a look that said we had more than exceeded our time. But what could I do? The two chiefs of state were thoroughly enjoying each other. Then Brzezinski jumped into the conversation. He brought up a book on the origins of man by the famous Jesuit anthropologist Teilhard de Chardin. They began to debate God's role in creating man, whether humans evolved or were created by God.

A strange conversation then developed between Brzezinski and Gairy, and they were pretty much in agreement about most things. Suddenly the Chief of Protocol broke in and said to me, "You know, there are other heads of state waiting out there." No one moved to leave. A little later Abelardo entered again, carrying the big purple box with a pink ribbon, which he placed in front of Sir Eric. This was supposed to be the cue that we had to go. To my bewilderment, Sir Eric said, "Oh, Mr. President. I wasn't expecting this from you. This is lovely. I don't know what to say." I leaned over and whispered to Sir Eric, "I think that's your present for the President." He said, "Are you sure?" I replied, "All I know is that I saw it in your hotel room so I think it's something you're giving to him." He said, "Oh," and he picked it up and he put it in front of Carter. "This is my present to you."

Carter was like a little kid, unwrapping the box. It was a hideous wrapping job, and beneath the paper was a Del Monte canned corn carton, inside of which were many famous spices from Grenada. "Oh, Roslyn will love this," Carter said. Sir Eric held up a jar to the President's nose and said, "Here, Mr. President, smell this nutmeg." Delighted, Carter went into his office next door and came back with a magnificent book of photographs of the earth from outer space, signed by all the astronauts. It was a gift to the President of the United States from the astronauts. Sir Eric almost cried. He was beaming over this marvelous book, and I thought, how could the president give that away? But Carter handed it over and he said, "Sir, we have so many things in common. This book shows how God sees us—and how our friends from outer space see us."

When finally our visit with Carter ended, the President led Sir Eric out past the restless chiefs of state who were waiting. He walked his guest clear to the curb, holding an umbrella over Sir Eric because it was raining. A photograph of Sir Eric getting into his limousine with Carter holding the umbrella over him was published all around the world. To have the U.S. president holding an umbrella over a black leader really struck a chord.

That conversation between Carter and Gairy was one of the most peculiar I witnessed in my time as a diplomat. I later asked Brzezinski if he remembered it and he said, "How could I possibly forget it?" In my memorandum of conversation, I reported simply that there was a general exchange of views with widespread agreement, a very pleasant meeting, etc. I never recorded what actually went on. To this day I'm not sure if Carter was acting or if he really had seen UFOs. I know his sister does say God talks to her but I shouldn't comment about the rest of what was said.

I did much more than bask in the tropical sun and deal with oddball leaders in Barbados. We faced many challenges, and one difficult experience in particular vexed me greatly. It put me in the middle of another crisis.

The situation began when there was a report that arms were being shipped from the United States into Grenada, hidden in barrels of grease. I immediately flew to Grenada to ask Sir Eric what was going on. He said the shipments were going to people in the New Jewel Movement, a Marxist group that was plotting to overthrow his government. He assured me that he had everything under control and insisted that I shouldn't worry. I questioned the British Commissioner about the arms. He confirmed that there was growing opposition in Grenada to Sir Eric in the form of a strong Marxist group. He said there was potential for violence but he couldn't say if it was imminent.

I reported to the State Department, where people were very unhappy about Sir Eric and the arms shipments. About that time, Sir Eric left for the U.S. to speak before the General Assembly of the United Nations. He was going to talk to them about how God told him what to do and what the people from outer space had said to him. I made it a point to see him as he passed through Barbados. Agents from the Bureau of Alcohol, Tobacco, and Firearms joined me in my meeting with him at the airport. They had come to investigate the arms shipments. After our meeting, Gairy flew to New York and the agents flew to Grenada. That very night the coup came.

Since Sir Eric was out of the country, he wasn't done in, but the New Jewel Movement took over the island. It then became my very difficult job to negotiate with them, trying to protect American interests. The new government was avowedly Marxist, and in no time the

Cubans put in an appearance. I was negotiating with Maurice Bishop, the new headman. He was a handsome young fellow whom I liked. We got along fine, even though he was a dedicated Marxist. The coup caused grave concern in the United States about the course events had taken. The New Jewel Movement represented another Soviet beachhead in the Caribbean.

I was about to leave Barbados for a new assignment, but received specific instructions for a serious talk with Bishop about Cuban arms and agents before I left. I was to tell him that such activity necessarily would lead to great problems in relations between the U.S. and Grenada. I was also to inform him of the economic support the U.S. was prepared to offer him. As I learned from my diplomatic mentors, I made sure to leave Bishop a "non-paper," which is not a formal note but a copy of the specific points I had made in carrying out Washington's instructions. My intention was to make sure that Bishop made no mistake as to what I had said.

To my surprise, many attacked me for giving Bishop that talking paper. A later report in the *Atlantic Monthly* and several other media outlets were critical of my actions.[7] I am confident I did the right thing. I was not the author of the points made to Bishop, although I supported them. In any case, the relationship between Grenada and the U.S. fell apart soon after our meeting. Bishop's pleasant mask came off.

I had decided to be the tough guy with Bishop because I was not certain that Bishop would take seriously my successor, an attractive young woman. I advised Bishop that the New Jewel Movement's involvement with Cuba and the Soviet Union could lead to a showdown with the U.S. At the time, though, there were about 400 American medical students studying in Grenada, and Bishop had them as de facto hostages, so I couldn't be too threatening. I didn't want to place the students in danger.

I took a lot of flack from people in the New Jewel Movement and their supporters in the U.S. A black congressman from Oakland

---

7. *Atlantic Monthly,* February 1984.

attacked me, saying that I didn't appreciate the fine people in power in Granada. I departed Granada soon after my conversations with Bishop, leaving behind many problems. In 1983, during the Reagan years, the U.S. sent military forces into Grenada to overthrow Bishop's successor, Bernard Coard—a real thug, who killed Maurice Bishop and took the government even farther to the extreme left. He, like Bishop, was a communist, but Coard was ruthless and violent.

I remember the Deputy of the CIA, Frank Carlucci, saying to me, "Frank, the Marxist coup happened on your watch. How did you allow that to happen?" I was also criticized about the way I handled my relationship with Bishop. For example, Ashley Hewitt, the director of the Office of Caribbean Affairs, called me and said, "Frank, in your reports to Washington you're calling Bishop and his people Marxists, and that's causing problems for us. People are really nervous about them and are afraid that you're exaggerating. Couldn't it be that these are good people who just wanted to get rid of that nut case Sir Eric Gairy?" I replied that I knew the New Jewel people personally and had no doubt they were Marxists. I told Hewitt that if he didn't want me to use that term, he should send me an instruction in writing. I refused to take instructions over the telephone. "Send me written instructions and I will call them progressives or Catholic liberals or whatever you want," I said. Those instructions never came.

Most of our leave-takings from posts were great. We usually departed as the toasts of the town, but not so with my departure from Barbados. I left Barbados with a reputation for being too hard-nosed, too tough. That was ironic because I needed all the toughness I could muster in my next assignment, the worst of my career, in Guatemala.

13

Guatemala: The Failure of a Mission

Guatemala is one of the loveliest countries in the world. Its people are kind, gentle, and hardworking to a fault. Their artistic abilities are unmatched and their cultural history is on a par with the great cultures of the world.

President Carter sent me to this lovely country in 1979. From the first day of my arrival I witnessed an ongoing tragedy. My posting there threw me into a cauldron of conflict. For twenty-some years a low grade civil war had been raging as far left groups fought to seize power. The Marxists believed violence was the only way to change a very iniquitous situation. The people who had money and property, the oligarchs, dominated a status quo they fought to maintain. They controlled the government. However the government also represented the middle-class and those in business, most of them young and interested in making the country work. The army was at war with the rebels. The police were ineffective or complicit in the kidnappings, murders, and massacres that were occurring. The church was divided on whom to support. It was a very nasty situation, but the State Department and the White House assured me of their confidence that I could do something to ameliorate the situation and assure U.S. interests were protected. I felt I had to make an especially good effort because Guatemala is a key country in Central America, a region of significant importance to U.S. security interests.

Just before I left Washington for my post, the mayor of Guatemala City, Manuel Colom Argüeta, was assassinated. He was progressive and very popular. I regret never having the opportunity to work with him. He was murdered just before I arrived. The following week, the commanding general of the army was assassinated in retribution. It was a very difficult situation to step into. Immediately upon my arrival, U.S. intelligence officers informed me that, as the American Ambassador, I was very close to the top of the list of targets for assassination. That was great news. We had already lost one Ambassador there, John Gordon Mein, who in 1968 was assassinated on his way to his office. He was traveling down the main boulevard of the city in light traffic. About four blocks from the embassy, a couple of cars cut him off and stopped him. His car was heavily armored, but he opened the door and tried to run to the protection of the embassy. The assassins shot him right there, on the main boulevard. Friends of ours who were just a few cars back of his described seeing his body lying there in the middle of the street, blood spreading on the pavement.

I was under no illusions when I arrived: Guatemala was a very dangerous place. Dolores came with me, but not the children. I initially thought the situation in Uruguay had been worse, but I soon changed my mind. Guatemala was at least as dangerous, maybe more so, given my high profile. I became used to traveling in a convoy, following a lead car that held a driver and three guards armed with machine guns. In the middle, my car was heavily armored with thick, bulletproof windows. A fellow with a pistol rode in the front seat of my sedan. The third car in the convoy carried three machine-gun-armed men.

The terrible situation in Guatemala seemed to be getting worse. It was very common for people I had just met to be murdered. In one case, the person I was supposed to meet, a leader of the Jewish community, was killed just an hour before our meeting time. It was more or less a situation of open warfare—not pitched battles in the capital city, but assassinations, kidnappings, and disappearances. In the north, in the Quiché region, the situation was even worse. Whole villages were being wiped out or displaced amid pitched battles between the insurgents and the military. The hapless villagers were caught in between. It was a miserable situation.

The president of Guatemala, Romeo Lucas Garcia, was handsome, tall, broad shouldered—sort of a John Barrymore type—but he was a cold-blooded, vicious man. He had eyes like a cobra, and when he fixed those eyes on you, it made you nervous. I'd tell him, "Mr. President, what's going on is not the way to solve the nation's problems. Your country's reputation is being ruined. Your policies make things worse. You must try to bring your citizens into a dialogue." He'd say, "Well, I'd expect that from you because you've just arrived. But the situation is beyond that. The only thing to do is crush those people by whatever means it takes." He always brushed me off and I lacked the leverage to force his will.

Dolores and I had been in Guatemala for only one week when we faced our first crisis. My secretary, a lovely Puerto Rican girl, informed me there were people calling on the phone who refused to identify themselves but insisted on talking to me. She was unsure if I wanted to be connected to callers like that or if she should just hang up. The callers insisted they'd only talk to me, so I took the call. A very cross voice, obviously a young person's, said, "You should know we've just kidnapped the Undersecretary of Foreign Affairs, Alonso Lima, and we will kill him unless you follow our instructions. Go to an empty house at such and such an address. In the mailbox are instructions that you must follow. As the new American Ambassador you better be sure you do what we tell you to do."

When they hung up I thought it must have been a crank call. I sent an assistant to the address, who found a message in the mailbox. The note said Vice-Minister Alonso Lima had just been kidnapped and would be killed unless I ran up a white flag over the embassy, demanded that the Guatemalan government release three specific comrades it was holding prisoner, and pressured the newspapers to publish the terrorists' manifesto. The note said if I did not do as instructed, Sr. Alonso Lima's blood would be on my hands.

This was my first week as Ambassador to Guatemala! I called the State Department to tell them I was in a pickle. They reminded me that I was not to give in to this sort of threat. When I asked, "What if they kill the man?" they said that would be the insurgents' doing, not mine. I felt trapped, and I decided to work for a compromise.

Dolores came up with a way to settle the flag problem. At the commissary she brought a big, bright pink pillowcase. We didn't run it up the main flagpole but we put it over the main entrance to the embassy. I went to the President and said, "*Señor* Presidente, they say they're going to kill Sr. Alonso Lima if I don't urge you to release three people that they say you are holding prisoner." He replied, "Well, we don't have them, and we don't know who or where they are. They've probably gone off to Cuba." It was probable the prisoners had been killed.

I talked with the editors of the major newspapers about the manifesto, but they refused to publish materials written by the insurgents. At this point I was certain the poor old Vice-Minister was doomed and I felt bad. I had done as much as I could. But fortunately, they didn't kill him. They held him for about 10 days and decided that I had tried to meet their demands and that he was such a gentle person that they let him go. I was greatly relieved and thanked Dolores for her pillow case idea.

That was my introduction to Guatemala, and it presaged things to come. The anxiety was constant. Twice during my year and a few months in Guatemala, the head of the CIA station took me into a secure room and said, "Ambassador, as you know, we have a penetration into the most dangerous of the terrorist groups in the country. They're planning to kill you tomorrow but you cannot in any way betray that we know that or it will compromise our sources. They don't want to take you as a hostage. They're going to kill you."

I knew my position was precarious and had already taken actions to protect myself. Every day I altered my departures from my residence. I would leave one morning at 6:00, one morning at 11:00, taking different routes to my office each day. The terrorists were reluctant to hang around for long periods in public places waiting to undertake their actions. This gave me some protection, but I was more than a bit nervous. I didn't tell Dolores, but I made sure that my will was written. I wrote little letters to the kids, not saying anything in particular, just sending loving words.

The day after my warning from the CIA, I increased my vigilance. I left home during the maximum traffic time, when the rush hour traffic was at its worst. I was sweating as we drove three cars into heavy traffic. Among the cars all around us, zipping and crowding for ways ahead, we didn't know if a hit team was waiting for us. Luckily, I made it to the embassy. That night, instead of coming home as I usually did at about seven, I left at one in the morning and sped home. Thankfully, no attempts were made on my life, but I was, in effect, a prisoner in my office and house. Fortunately, the residence had a huge garden, and I whiled away my hours in "captivity" by tending to it.

All my efforts to calm the violence in Guatemala proved unsuccessful. It didn't help that soon after I arrived, the U.S. government, in reaction to a terrible series of killings, cut off assistance to Guatemala. Military assistance had been cut long before. This made it very difficult for me to exercise any leverage over the government. Since I wasn't getting anywhere in reining in the military, I thought a good approach would be to try to emphasize whatever positive things we could find. We did have a program of training the Guatemalans to grow world-class flowers that they could export, for example, and we worked with artisans to improve handicrafts for export. Dolores did very well at helping gain acceptance across the political spectrum, which is very important. We did feel that we were accomplishing something, in spite of the terrible political climate.

I came up with an idea for a way to gain more influence over the warring factions. I reasoned that if a group of countries banded together and acted more or less as a unit, it might have more clout than any one country alone. To this end, diplomats from several countries, and other interested parties formed an organization we called the Paella Club. Paella is a rice dish that Spaniards make. It's the type of production that everybody participates in: someone peels the shrimp, another chops the pork up in cubes, another prepares the shellfish, and someone cooks the rice and arranges the garnishes. It makes for a great dish. We envisioned our group as participating in a similar way, each person offering a suggestion for ways to influence Guatemalan politics.

The Paella Club included the Ambassador of Venezuela, who had some clout because Guatemala was dependent on Venezuelan oil; the Ambassador of Costa Rica, who had great influence among the intelligentsia, the students, the universities, and the intellectuals; the Ambassador of Spain, who was newly arrived; and some Christian Democratic leaders. We got together about every two weeks to cook paella, taking turns as hosts of the meetings. It was all a cover for what was really a political action group. It showed great promise as a concept.

Terrible events were commonplace in Guatemala, but one in particular affected me directly. On January 30, 1980, as I was having lunch downtown, a call summoned me to the embassy. When I arrived, I learned that a terrorist group had occupied the Spanish Embassy. For several days previous, a group of campesinos, or peasants, had been trying to occupy schools and embassies to demand the release of imprisoned members of their group. They were also calling for an end to the terrible bloodshed in the Quiché. The campesino activists, dressed in their colorful native clothing, were joined by young university students and a Roman Catholic nun. Their group numbered twelve or thirteen altogether.

The U.S. Embassy was triply protected and it was almost impossible for people to break into our place, but the Spanish Ambassador, Máximo Cajal, maintained an open-door policy. This openness proved a liability on the day his embassy was occupied. It so happened that on that day he had arranged that the former vice president and former foreign minister of Guatemala meet him in his office. When the protestors took over the embassy, they inadvertently took hostage not only the Ambassador and all the diplomatic staff of the embassy, but also two of the most prominent men in Guatemala.

The protestors demanded that the government release their comrades and stop the warfare in the north. What happened next is a matter of debate, with several versions told and retold. One account says that a secretary called the police when she saw the protestors rush in and begin herding everybody into the Ambassador's office. She sounded the alarm and the police arrived. Ambassador Cajal denies the police were called but confirms he insisted that they go away. He felt that they could do nothing about the situation, and in any case they were violating diplomatic immunity by entering the embassy precinct. He preferred to try to talk the occupiers into leaving.

The police paid no attention to the Ambassador, who was in his office with the door locked. They began chopping down the door with fire axes so they could confront the intruders. At that point, the "peaceable" peasants and students pulled out Molotov cocktails and guns and began shooting at the door. As the door crashed down, the Ambassador was in front of the group yelling to the police and ordering them to leave. At that moment, one of the protestors tried to throw a Molotov cocktail through the door at the police. Unfortunately, the cocktail hit the doorjamb and bounced back into the room, where it exploded.

Thirty-nine people burned to death in that room. There were only two survivors. One was the Ambassador, who, because he was in front of the group, leapt through the flames and escaped. He was burned from head to toe, however. Under the pile of bodies, one of the young peasants also survived the fire while everybody around him was turned to near charcoal.

All I had to do was turn on the television to see all this unfolding. I saw the Spanish Ambassador wander out of the building in a daze, burnt from head to toe, his clothes hanging on him. Nobody seemed to recognize him. Those of us watching at the U.S. embassy wanted to help. I sent the number two man of the embassy, Mel Sinn, to see what he could do. Arriving in our armored limousine, he ensured that the Ambassador was placed in an ambulance and taken to a hospital immediately.

Soon after the tragedy, the Papal Nuncio, who was the dean of the diplomatic corps, called together the diplomatic chiefs in Guatemala City to decide how to respond to the situation. In addition to the horrible loss of life, there was great concern among us because the police and protestors had infringed on an embassy's inviolability. We discussed ideas for preventing similar hostage-takings at other embassies and for ensuring that the police respect diplomatic immunity.

As we were meeting, about 8:00 in the morning, the Costa Rican Ambassador rushed in, pale as a ghost. He reported that a group of armed men had just broken into the hospital, intent on killing the Ambassador and the other survivor of the embassy fire. He had been in Ambassador Cajal's room when he saw armed people running up and down the halls, looking for Cajal. He threw the sheets over Cajal and when the rebels ran into the room with pistols drawn, he gestured toward the shrouded Cajal, bowing his head as if he had just lost a loved one. The gunmen turned and ran out. Unfortunately, they did find the other survivor, whom they took to the university and shot. They put a sign around his neck that read "Executed for Terrorism."

The Ambassadors agreed that we had to save Cajal. There were people in his hospital room, but they were unarmed. I suggested that we bring the Ambassador to my residence because it was amply protected. The Venezuelan Ambassador drove his big white Cadillac to the hospital, snuck Cajal out, and delivered him to my house. Staying with us at the time were our close friends from Santa Fe, Antonio Taylor and his wife Matiana, and the former U.S. Ambassador to Spain, Bob Woodward. They gave up their rooms for Cajal, whom we put in a bathtub full of ice as soon as he arrived. We immediately called the doctors, who put ointments on him and wrapped him up like a mummy. He looked awful but kept asking, "What about my people?" I finally told him that all had died, even the poor cook who had only come to collect her salary. But I assured Cajal that he, at least, was safe.

By making a few phone calls, I located an excellent burn unit at Tulane University in New Orleans. I offered to have Cajal flown there right away, but the Spanish government had already dispatched a team to take care of him. That night, as we sat watching horrendous replays of the days' events on television, machine gun fire sprayed the front of our residence with bullets fired from the street. We dove for the floor, afraid the bullets would come through the windows. Once the firing stopped, Tony Taylor and I ran outside because I was sure some of the residence guards had been killed, but fortunately they were unharmed.

Many Spaniards arrived to help Cajal and after five days the Spanish government transported him to Spain. He was hospitalized in

Madrid, but even there the government posted a guard outside his hospital room. In 2000, Cajal published a book compiling the recollections of those involved in the tragedy, mine included.[8]

As the day's events had unfolded, I sent messages advising the State Department of my response to the crisis. The Department authorized me to do whatever I felt was necessary, and I did what I thought was right. Nonetheless there were repercussions for me. Many in Guatemala—especially the families of the two prominent men who were burned alive in the embassy—objected to me acting to save the Spanish Ambassador. They claimed the Ambassador had lured important people into the embassy so they would be taken hostage, and believed that Cajal should have died alongside their loved ones. To make things worse, the Guatemalan government claimed I had taken sides when I should have stayed out of the fray. I replied that I had done what any decent human being would do and didn't regret it.

The King of Spain knighted me for my actions in saving Ambassador Cajal, but controversy within Guatemala over my actions made the rest of my stay there more difficult. After the incident, I was identified with anti-government groups, which caused me to lose what little influence I had with hard-core government officials. The situation became progressively worse with time. The State Department informed me that President Carter disagreed with my stance on the deteriorating situation in the country. He thought that I should be more openly confrontational with the country's leaders and make strong public demands of them. I replied that I felt equally strongly that since I had no real leverage over the government or the military, confrontation would only force those with the most firepower into a dangerous corner, which would lead to more bloodshed. Rather than be confrontational, I argued that we should seek means to pressure, entice, and persuade the people in power that it was in their own best interests to stop the terrible bloodshed. I said that if they gave me

8. *¡Saber Quién Puso Fuego Allí!*, Madrid, Ediciones Melita

some time, I could try to accomplish that, but I flatly refused to carry out the confrontational policy they wanted.

My position didn't go over very well in Washington, so the Department of State sent a Deputy Assistant Secretary of State, Jim Cheek, to second me. Cheek was from Arkansas, was a very brash, archetypical southerner with a loud voice, a southern drawl, and a poor grasp of Spanish—although he thought he spoke it fluently. The State Department's message was, "Look, Ortiz, you don't have the balls to carry out our tough policy, so we're sending Jim down to do it for you." I said, "All right. Let him try."

Sending Cheek down was a slap in the face to me, but I conscientiously gathered together the key people to meet with him. First we had a small dinner with the cardinal archbishop, who wielded great power, former president Lagarud, who also was a power broker, a couple of the generals, and the foreign minister. Cheek read the riot act to them saying, "You're all killers. You've got to stop this," and so on. The cardinal said, "Are you including me in this?" And Cheek said, "We've talked to the Pope, and he is opposed to what's going on here." At that, the archbishop stood up at the table—I thought he was going to overturn my table as he rose—and he thundered, "I am the Pope's representative. I speak for the Pope here; you do not." He stomped out and the others followed suit, politely saying it was not a constructive evening. When I pointed out to Cheek that the evening had not been a success, he answered, "Well, it's better than the way you do things." I had to agree it was quite different, but I wasn't sure it was any better.

The next day I convened at my residence a large group that included many of the most important business leaders, bankers, the media, and intellectuals who really ran the country. Cheek informed them that he was delivering a message directly from the government of the United States, not through me as an intermediary, so that they could hear it straight. As he delivered his judgmental, tough message, he made an unfortunate mistake in his usage of Spanish. He said, "What Guatemala needs is '*un gobierno popular.*'" In Spanish, that generally means a "people's" or Marxist government. He thought he was saying that Guatemala needed a democratic, popular government, but in fact his audience heard him advocating a Marxist government. He compounded this by saying a form of socialism was necessary in Guatemala. This message caused a lot of consternation. Most of his listeners were furious with him and left the meeting enraged, defiant, and not cowed in the least. Cheek had inflamed the situation.

Cheek went back to Washington and reported he had read the riot act to the Guatemalans, telling them exactly what they had to do. I, on the other hand, reported that his effort was terribly counterproductive and would have an effect opposite to what we wanted. I warned that even more blood would flow.

Just about the time Cheek left, our embassy received notice that an American warship, the USS Manley, would visit ports in the Caribbean as a demonstration of the American commitment to security in the region. I was asked to approve a visit, which I did. I believed we should flex some muscle. Some in Washington thought it outrageous to fly an American flag in a country of such terrible killers. I received heavy public criticism in the U.S. for approving the Manley's visit.

This was the final straw for me. I informed my superiors in Washington that I simply could not do what they wanted me to do. Congressman (later Senator) Tom Harkin of Iowa attacked me in a letter to the State Department. The Department offered no defense. The administration clearly was not happy with my approach. It was abundantly clear it was time to end my ambassadorship. The State Department had already reached the same conclusion, and I was relieved of my post.

From Guatemala, I was posted as the chief political advisor, with the rank of Ambassador, to the Commander in Chief of the Southern Command in Panama City. After my departure, the White House assigned as Ambassador to Guatemala a hard-nosed former Ambassador to Chile. The Carter administration wanted him to carry out the heavy-handed, confrontational program that I refused to deploy. Not surprisingly, the Guatemalan government refused to accept him or any American Ambassador for quite a while. During that time, the ruthless President Lucas Garcia was overthrown by someone even more brutal, General Rios Montt. Worse massacres followed, just as I predicted. The U.S. had no control. We had lost all leverage whatsoever. Even reasonable, moderate Guatemalans seemed to be in favor of the mass elimination of political dissidents. In 1981–83, the Guatemalan military killed tens of thousands of mostly innocent campesinos before those having power were finally convinced that mass slaughter did not serve anyone's best interest. The policy I recommended—of multilateral, strong, steady, quiet pressure—came too late for those thousands of victims. However, with strong international pressure, a viable peace eventually was achieved and free and fair elections were held. I served as an international observer of the national election held in the late 1980s. In 1996 there was a peace accord signed that so far has held.

Our departure from Guatemala was beautiful in many ways, in spite of the circumstances. Friends rallied from all sides, showering us with gifts and affection. Overall, my experience in Guatemala was extremely sad and unhappy, although to this day I am remembered very favorably there. I visit Guatemala often. My daughter, Tina, lived there for five years. The Guatemalans are wonderful to me. Some say, "You were right. Too bad they didn't listen to you." I find some consolation in that kindness but find no satisfaction in the vindication.

Signing the Base Agreement with Spain, 1963,
with Secretary of State Rusk and General Curtis LeMay

My wife Dolores

Nodding acquaintance with the Queen of England

Sir Eric Gairy, Prime Minister of Grenada

Presenting credentials as U.S. Ambassador to Guatemala, 1979

Eye-to-eye with the fearsome President of Guatemala,
Romeo Lucas García

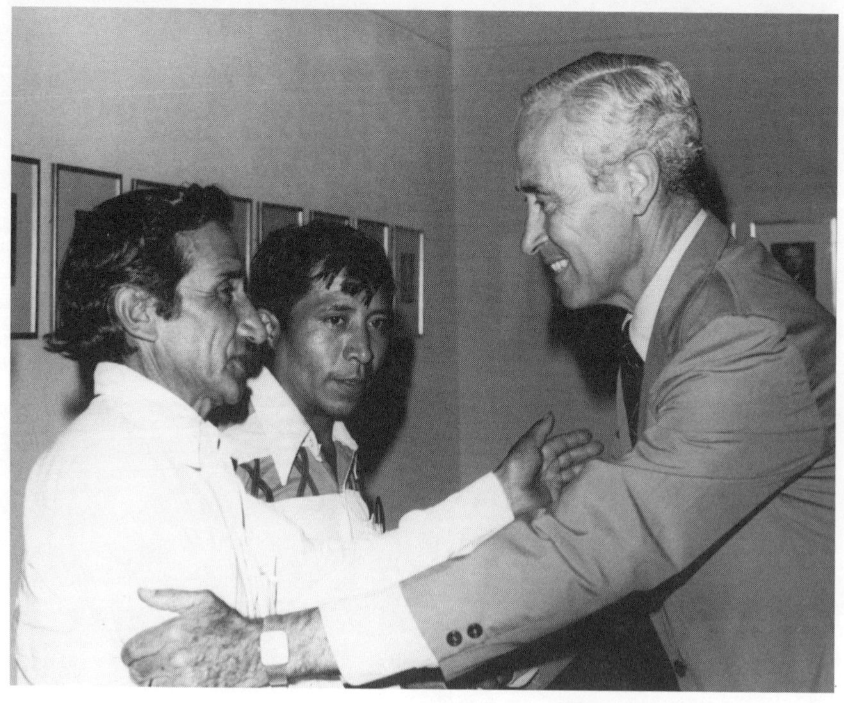

Receiving Indian leaders, Guatemala

14

Panama to Peru: A Tropical Interlude and a Contentious Return

The next stop in my career was Panama City. Dolores and I had never lived in so tropical a place. The humidity and heat were so constant and oppressive that we had to keep light bulbs lit next to our shoes and clothes to keep them from molding. It was a far cry from the pleasant highlands of Guatemala.

At Southern Command headquarters I was assigned a large office and worked with a wonderful commanding general, Wallace Nutting, who was responsible for U.S. military affairs in all of Latin America. Nutting listened to and respected my opinions. We worked with the U.S. military attachés in Latin American countries, directing our efforts at using intelligence operations and military assistance to counteract the growing Marxist attempts to take over Latin American governments. This was a threat not everyone in the U.S. considered serious, but our intelligence reports moved us to be somewhat alarmed.

Soon after arriving I found that the Southern Command headquarters in Panama City, like Washington, D.C., was equipped with a tunnel into a mountainside, at Quarry Heights, to serve as a shelter in the event of a nuclear attack. We could sprint from the Southern Command headquarters across to the shelter in 30 seconds.

I had no official responsibilities in the Republic of Panama, the border of which lay a stone's throw away from our headquarters. The assignment to SouthCom, as it was called, was a good one for me, offering interesting work. Thankfully, we had no security problems. We drove our own car and lived in our own private residence. We didn't need bodyguards and my children could safely visit. We found the military life very pleasant. We felt welcomed and were able to accomplish many positive things during our one-year stay.

During my assignment to SouthCom, Ronald Reagan was elected President, with George H. W. Bush Vice President. A few days after the election, I came back from lunch to find my officemates very excited. The Vice President-elect had called from Houston and asked to talk to me right away. Surprised, I promptly returned the call. Mr. Bush said he wanted me to come work for him as his foreign policy advisor. He had chosen an admiral to be his military advisor and wanted me as his foreign policy advisor. I requested a personal meeting with Mr. Bush to discuss his offer, and he invited me to his transition office in Washington in a couple of weeks.

Soon after I received the call from Vice President-elect Bush, the American Ambassador in Panama, Ambler Moss, called to say General Torrijos wanted to meet with me immediately. Omar Torrijos, a very influential general, had succeeded in getting the Panama Canal back from the U.S. when Jimmy Carter was president. Torrijos was a crude and tough guy who openly derided Americans. He counted among his close friends the English writer Graham Greene and Fidel Castro. Apparently, Torrijos had been tapping our phones or had otherwise become aware of the call from Bush, which explained his wanting to meet with me right away. Ambassador Moss felt that since he was the U.S. Ambassador to Panama, he should accompany me to see Torrijos. I had no idea what Torrijos wanted and welcomed Moss's company.

We flew in a military aircraft to El Farallon on the Pacific coast north of Panama City, where Torrijos owned a big house. Ambler and I arrived early in the morning, dressed in our best clothes. We were escorted up to the house and then onto the terrace, where Torrijos lay reclining in a hammock, wearing only his underpants—boxers, gaping boxers. He had a big belly and mounds of ruddy skin. He looked like a big walrus rocking back and forth on the hammock.

I'd never seen nor had anything to do with Torrijos and was taken aback by his appearance, but Ambler was not surprised. Torrijos said, "Draw closer," and to his attendant, "Give them chairs." Then, with his bare feet more or less in my face, he said, "I've heard about you. You are Reagan's man in Panama now." "I wouldn't say that," I demurred, "I'm assigned to General Nutting." Torrijos protested, "No, no. Don't pretend. We know who you are. And I want you to deliver important messages to Reagan. I want the new U.S. government to understand what we're going to do here." I said, "I think you're wrong. Mr. Moss is the American Ambassador and he's the one that will transmit—"Don't give me that stuff," Torrijos interrupted. "I know who you are and I want you to deliver my messages."

Torrijos fixed his attention on me, saying, "Don't worry about the future of the canal. Don't try to stop the transfer." Then he abruptly stopped to interject, "I know that your people have this place bugged and they're listening to what we're saying, so I'm going to break this off and take you to a place where I can't be heard by your people." I told him he was exaggerating, but he insisted, "No, no. Don't kid me. I know."

Torrijos called for a helicopter, then dressed himself. When the helicopter arrived, Moss, Torrijos, and I boarded, along with a woman and a man who seemed to be Torrijos' assistants. We flew over the middle of Panama and abruptly put down in a clearing on top of a jungle-shrouded mountain. The helicopter left us there. It was hot, especially for Moss and me in our coats and ties, and the ground was muddy from recent rain. Torrijos grinned, "This is a place where the American intelligence cannot track us. And this is what I want you to tell Reagan."

Torrijos then began a long monologue, mostly puffery. I tried my best to follow his convoluted and endless message. Moss was sweating profusely. We began walking down the mountainside, wading in the mud, and we walked and walked and walked through the jungle with

Torrijos all the while saying, "Tell Reagan this and tell Reagan that . . . we're going to need money for this and the Chinese want that and we've got a free port . . ." And he often added, with emphasis, "You've got to get it right to the new government." We were covered with mud and plastered with sweat when finally we came to a road with a hard surface of base course. Walking down the road, Torrijos' assistant made a call on his radio, and a jeep soon came along and picked us up. Torrijos told us he was taking us to a place called Las Palmeras.

Along the way, where the road followed a beautiful river, Torrijos ordered the driver to stop. He said, "Look at you guys. You're a mess." Well, we were. I'd rolled my pants up, but they were still covered with mud. "Let's go for a swim," Torrijos suggested, and before we knew it, he had taken off his clothes and jumped into the river. I thought, "I don't think I want to do that!" But I did take off my shoes to clean them and washed my feet, face and hands. The Ambassador did the same as we waited for Torrijos to finish his swim. When he emerged from the river and dried himself off with his shirt, we continued down the road.

Finally, around noon, we arrived at some buildings where two very pretty girls were waiting. Torrijos told us the women were school teachers, adding, "You know I believe in education." I said, "That's wonderful. I think you should." Then he pointed to the women and asked, "Which one do you like?" "I beg your pardon?" I replied. He said, "Pick one and take her upstairs." I declined, saying, "Well, thank you very much, but no thanks," and the Ambassador also declined. Torrijos then announced that he would send off to Panama City for whatever kind of food I wanted. He asked what was my favorite restaurant and I named a great seafood place.

A plane took off and came back shortly with a fine lunch, which we shared with the two teachers. When it started raining heavily Torrijos said, "Come on, now. There are two rooms for you upstairs and the ladies will be very happy to accompany you." I told him I'd just watch the rain. Torrijos announced he was going to take a nap, as he always did after lunch, and went upstairs. Ambler and I sat on the porch and watched the rain fall. We told the two teachers they should get back to their classes.

Finally we were told the general was ready for us. "Where are we going?" we asked. "Upstairs," was the only reply. Upstairs we found Torrijos lying on a big bed with four little seven- or eight-year-old girls. They were watching a cartoon video on television. Torrijos had reverted to his underpants-only attire. He said, "Aren't they cute?" We agreed that they were cute, but I felt sick. I don't know what was going on. Maybe nothing. But certainly it didn't look right.

Torrijos said he'd decided to take us to Contadora Island, offshore of Panama in the Pacific. I told the general that he must understand that Ambassador Moss would transmit his ideas to the new government in the United States and that we really had to get back to Panama City. By now it was about four or five in the afternoon and my wife thought I was going to be gone for only a couple hours. But Torrijos would have none of it. He said, "No, no. We're not through. I want you to meet Gabriel Lewis, my chief foreign policy advisor. And he's on Contadora."

The rain was still pouring down as we climbed into an airplane and took off. Torrijos, who was terribly afraid of flying, carried a bottle of whiskey with him. (He was killed in an airplane crash years later.) Torrijos took big swigs of the bourbon as we flew from Las Palmeras to Contadora Island—a very fancy place where the Shah of Iran stayed at the beginning of his exile. Gabriel Lewis had a dinner waiting for us at the luxury hotel on the island. I knew something of Lewis, a Panamanian businessman with flawless English and a wide knowledge of the U.S. He acted as advisor and maybe bagman for Torrijos. He was a very smart man.

Torrijos began his harangue again: "You know, it's your job to let President Reagan know the true situation in Panama," drilling me again on the same daylong message. By this time it was dark. Moss and I reminded Torrijos that nobody knew our whereabouts and that we must get back to Panama City. But Torrijos said there were no lights at the airstrip, so no plane could take off after dark. Incredulous, we asked if he intended for us to spend the night there. He said, yes, that he had suites for us in the hotel. No problem—for him.

We protested that we weren't at all prepared to spend the night, but he said not to worry. We were each shown to a luxury suite equipped with toothbrushes, razors, and pajamas. All this time, Dolores and the people back at headquarters in Panama City, not knowing our whereabouts, were becoming frantic. We had been incommunicado for the entire day and they were still under the illusion that we were in Farallon. But we had no choice but to stay, and we managed to enjoy a pleasant and uneventful evening.

The next morning, we woke to find Torrijos gone. He had just disappeared, without so much as a good-bye. Gabriel Lewis took up his droning, however, reminding me one more time, "Now remember, Frank, you are our direct channel to Reagan." I repeated my worn-out response, and then we finally flew back to Panama City.

I flew to Washington to meet with Vice-president-elect Bush shortly after my experience with General Torrijos, but I only related the gist of Torrijos' messages. In fact, I didn't relate the weird details of my strange experience to anyone in Washington. They would have thought I was on drugs.

When I met with Mr. Bush at his transition office on Lafayette Square, I respectfully declined his offer of a position on his staff. I wanted to say this to him directly and personally: I could not afford to come back to Washington to serve as his advisor. I explained to him that the rent from our house in Washington, combined with money we saved by living on an army post, allowed me to pay my four children's college tuitions. I thanked him and he expressed his disappointment. He graciously added that he understood our circumstances. It was a very difficult moment for me. I realize now that that may not have been the smartest thing to do, because, of course, he later became president. If I'd been his chief foreign affairs advisor, presumably I would have had a high rank in his government. But in any case it was very flattering to be asked and whenever I see him and in our correspondence, ex-President Bush still refers to his invitation and how close we came to working together in Washington.

I then returned to Panama. I'd been there not quite a year when the word came of a new assignment, to Peru. We were overjoyed. I had served in Peru before, but this would be my first time as Ambassador there. Lima and Peru have always been among our favorite places. My old colleague, President Belaunde Terry, who was overthrown by the coup in 1968, had been re-elected to office. We were close friends, which was one reason President Reagan chose to post me there.

Dolores and I were thrilled to be returning to Peru, but we arrived in Lima to a mixed reception. Some of the media, especially the liberal press, dug up the old, disproved charge that, as "head of the CIA" I had plotted to assassinate President Velasco Alvarado and speculated that I was head of the CIA in Latin America. The political left was very critical of my appointment, saying that it was a bad idea to name me as the new Ambassador. A negative story to that effect appeared in the *Washington Post,* eliciting my immediate rebuttal. I demanded to know where the *Post*'s Lima correspondent found her sources of information for so negative a story. I enclosed with my letters the text of official statements by the president and foreign minister of Peru, who both said they looked forward to my return and were delighted I would be U.S. Ambassador. *The Post*'s report had said nothing about their welcome. After months of wavering, the Post printed a very rare, formal apology for the story and their reporting.[9] The editor and publisher were also very accommodating, admitting that the *Post* was wrong and that the Peruvian government had in fact welcomed me with open arms. Furthermore, they made it clear that the previous accusations of my involvement in an assassination plot were malicious and false. That silenced my critics in the local press.

During our two-plus years in Peru, we began a mission to draw the Peruvians together to improve their economic situation. Towards the middle of the second year, in about 1982, we began receiving reports of a terrorist group forming in Ayacucho in the highlands of Peru. It became apparent that these brutal, ideologically driven Maoists would stop at nothing to destabilize the country. For example, they were determined to undermine efforts at economic development in the highlands,

---

9. *Washington Post,* January 7, 1981, "It Is Unfair to the Ambassador." This and other documents relating to my career can be found in my papers, archived in the Fray Angélico Chávez History Library.

where we supported breeding stations for the finest alpaca, llama, and vicuña specimens. Our goal was to develop the finest wool-producing animals. We helped build a wonderful station, with the support of experts in animal husbandry from the European Union. The terrorists broke into the facility, slaughtered all the animals, and burned the facilities to the ground. It was a clear demonstration of the group's ruthlessness—and this was just the beginning of their terrorist activities. They called themselves the *Sendero Luminoso,* the Shining Path.

I knew that Peru had the potential to be one of the richest agricultural producers in the world. Where water is available, fine, long-fiber cotton grows well. The country produces the best pineapples I've every tasted, as well as wonderful fruits of all kinds, and large quantities of sugar cane. You name it, Peruvians can grow it. Unfortunately, commercial production of these valuable crops was hampered by many factors. A major hindrance was the fact that the leftist military government in 1968 had expropriated most large landholdings and incorporated them into unproductive communal farms, which seriously damaged the agricultural sector.

I invited Clayton Yeutter, who later served as Secretary of Agriculture but at the time was head of the Chicago Mercantile Exchange, to Peru. I asked him and his team of experts to advise Peruvians on how to improve agricultural production. These and other efforts to revitalize the sector were very successful. (The head of the Peruvian agricultural college at the time was an intelligent Japanese Peruvian named Fujimori, who in 1990 became president.)

In April 1982, the Falklands Island War erupted when the Argentine military junta made the great mistake of invading the islands, which were British territory. I had had dinner with the junta leader, General Galtieri, in Panama a couple years before the invasion took place. Galtieri was a ruddy, blustering, hard-driving character who expressed little regard for British Prime Minister Margaret Thatcher—or for anyone else. The Argentine public turned out en masse to support the invasion. Latin Americans, except for the Chileans, rallied to support Argentina. The atmosphere was wild and unthinking. When the U.S. stood by the British and Prime Minister Thatcher sent in military forces to expel the

Argentines, the early exuberance wavered and turned to active hostility toward the U.S.

I was honored when Peruvian President Belaunde Terry asked for my collaboration in his efforts to stop the Falkland War. I spent many hours in the presidential palace, working on texts for a cease-fire to which the British and Argentines would agree. I was on the telephone with Secretary of State Alexander Haig and a British representative in Washington. My primary contribution in these efforts was to cobble together words that, both in Spanish and English, would be acceptable in a joint, bilingual agreement.

By this time Peru had sent fighter planes and air-to-surface missiles to Argentina. The fighting was bloody and getting more serious by the day. The Latin American media were mauling the U.S. and its interests, but in Peru I believe my efforts spared the U.S. some of the venom being spilled against us elsewhere in the hemisphere.

After long negotiations it seemed we had a joint statement for a cease-fire that the two warring parties could accept. When it was submitted for final approval, I was very tired but pleased. President Belaunde Terry's exuberance got the better of him, and he called me to the palace for a press conference announcing the success of his efforts. His decision to announce a peace settlement so soon surprised me. I attended but warned him that it would have been better for the agreement to be signed and sealed, with the first announcements coming from London and Buenos Aires. My comments annoyed Belaunde Terry, as my suggested course of action would have diminished his role in the settlement.

As Belaunde Terry and I were announcing a peace accord, a British submarine torpedoed the Argentine warship Belgrano, resulting in heavy loss of life. Our carefully crafted agreement imploded and British military might, instead of diplomacy, settled the conflict. Mrs. Thatcher wanted no part of protracted diplomatic negotiations to settle sovereignty over the Falklands.

Galtieri and his colleagues were overthrown following the Falklands debacle. The Argentines were humiliated to a dangerous degree, while Margaret Thatcher won British hearts as the "Iron Lady."

In the aftermath of the conflict, the British press and an insistent and demanding member of Parliament from the Labor Party pursued me relentlessly. They sought confirmation that Ms. Thatcher had deliberately ordered the sinking of the Belgrano to destroy the Peruvian peace initiative. Having experience with U.S. political infighting, I had no interest in getting involved in British feuding. It took me months to shake off my pursuer from the Labor Party.

On the whole, our second tour in Peru was extremely successful. Towards the end of my second year there, I received a call from Judge Bill Clark, who was National Security Advisor for the President. On the secure phone, he said, "Frank, President Reagan would like you to go to Spain. Would you like that?" I said, "I'd die for it!" He said the steps would begin for a posting in Madrid. Dolores and I said goodbye to our beloved Peru and prepared for a new adventure. We left Peru amid demonstrations of great affection. I was giddy at the prospect of being New Mexico's Ambassador to what we sometimes call "the Mother Country."

A send-off to Peru by President Reagan

A warm welcome by President Belaunde Terry of Peru, 1981

With President Belaunde Terry announcing
a short-lived truce in the Falkland's War, 1982

Chatting with an Indian Chief, Amazonas, Peru

Tourism with my ex-boss, Henry Kissinger, Peru, 1982

Fourth of July reception, Lima, Peru

15

Argentina: The Pinnacle of a Career

My giddiness over an appointment to Spain lasted only a few weeks. While in Spain on a discreet exploratory visit, we traveled to Granada to tour the southern part of the country. Very early one morning the telephone rang. It was the White House, conveying a question from President Reagan: Would I object to going to Argentina instead of Spain? It seemed that the White House had another candidate for Madrid.

The administration in Washington was aware I had a good personal relationship with Italo Luder, the candidate expected to win upcoming elections for the presidency of Argentina. I had come to know Luder and Argentine politics during my time at the State Department's Southern Cone office, when Luder was a senator.

My reply to the White House was that of course I would do whatever the president wanted; Argentina would be a wonderful assignment. My acceptance meant that an ambassadorship in Spain dropped by the wayside, but it turned out for the best. Argentina became the pinnacle of my career.

I was fully aware that an assignment to Argentina would be very difficult. Just about a year before, their defeat in the Falklands War had tremendously humiliated Argentina, a country of very proud people.

The Argentine populace is almost entirely a blend of various European nationalities. The ethnic mixtures are very handsome. The women celebrate being women; the men celebrate being men. It's a very vibrant country, full of people of considerable self-confidence.

Their defeat in the Falklands War had been a great source of dishonor for the Argentines, whose invasion to occupy the islands had been thwarted by Maggie Thatcher—with American assistance. The war poisoned the relationship between the United States and Argentina. As a matter of fact, the Argentines at the time hated Americans more than they did the British who had defeated them.

Dolores and I experienced Argentine anti-American sentiment well before our arrival there in 1983. While we were immersed in preparations for our mission, a good friend gave us a formal dinner attended by about twenty people. During a lull in the dinner conversation, an Argentine woman said, "Frank, maybe you'd like to hear the latest joke in Buenos Aires?" I said, "Well, tell me, by all means. I want to keep up to date with the jokes." "During the Falklands War," she said, "there was a private who was in a foxhole next to his captain. The private said, 'Sir, I have both a British soldier and an American advisor in my gun sight. Whom should I kill first?' The officer's reply was, 'Shoot the American. It's pleasure before duty.'"

The people at the table thought this funny, but I didn't; I considered it an insult, but didn't make it an issue. Nevertheless, it presaged our reception in Argentina.

In terms of natural and human resources, Argentina rates as one of the richest countries in the world, but it has never been able to achieve its potential. The Argentines have a habit of self defeat. They never seem able to work together. In 1983, however, we were nevertheless hopeful that the imminent return to democracy would put Argentina on the right track.

When we arrived in Buenos Aires, the Argentine press was in full cry at the airport, of course. They swarmed over me like locusts with flash bulbs going off after we went through the official reception ceremonies. They peppered me with questions about how the United States would remedy its betrayal of Argentina. I said that Dolores and

I would do our very best to assure that good relations between the U.S. and Argentina, essential for the prosperity and security of both countries, were not compromised.

Just a couple of weeks after we arrived in Buenos Aires, Alfonsín—not Luder—assumed the presidency, ending the rule of the last military chief, General Reynaldo Bignone. The city of Buenos Aires—the whole country, in fact—went wild over the return of democracy. Vice President Bush arrived in Buenos Aires as the head of an American delegation to Alfonsín's inaugural. He and Mrs. Bush stayed with us. The anti-American sentiment was still strong then, and the Bush's visit called for heightened security at the embassy. We closed the big steel shutters on all the windows, Bush and his wife were not to use the elevator, all the servants were checked, and Secret Service agents were stationed throughout the embassy. When we appeared in public in the embassy's limousine, flying the American flag, people spat and threw rocks at us. I accompanied Vice President Bush—who is the most astonishing man I've ever known when it comes to varied but strong personal relationships—as he met with world leaders who had also flown in for the inauguration from all corners of the globe.

Among many other events, we had scheduled a meeting between Bush and the prime minister of Portugal. It was supposed to take place at my residence, but we were trapped inside the president of Argentina's residence, the Casa Rosada. We couldn't leave because great mobs cheering Alfonsín surrounded the residence. Our cars couldn't even get to the portico, so Vice President Bush decided we'd just have our meetings there in the Casa Rosada.

The encounter with the Portuguese prime minister was particularly important because at the time there were problems in Angola and Mozambique. We had to talk turkey to the prime minister. When it became clear we couldn't leave the Casa Rosada, Vice President Bush said to me, "Frank, find a secure place for us to meet with the Portuguese."

Every place I looked in the Casa Rosada was full of people, but it wasn't my house, so I couldn't just order people out of rooms. Frustrated in my attempts, I finally suggested to the Vice President that we meet in the only private space I could find—the men's room. And that's what we did: we went into the men's room and locked the door. The Portuguese prime minister and Bush had their meeting, during which we informed the prime minister that the U.S. would continue supporting Savimbi in Angola against the Marxist government. In the middle of the discussion, we heard the toilet flush and the Japanese Ambassador walked out from a stall. We were shocked that he had been listening to the conversation. That's how ridiculous things became in the jubilant commotion of Buenos Aires in 1983.

The Falklands War was only the most recent event in years of turbulence in Argentina. Beginning in 1975, Argentina suffered an internal war between the far left and the far right, with especially terrible consequences. After a series of unchecked assaults, kidnappings, bombings, and other forms of violence perpetuated by Marxist terrorist organizations, the hapless government of Isabelita Perón was overthrown. In March 1976, a military junta took power and immediately embarked on the infamous "dirty war" to crush the threat from the far left.

The Argentine military was pitiless in its efforts to stamp out what many considered a dangerous threat to the nation's security. Between 1976 and 1979, some nine thousand individuals, many of them idealistic youths, were abducted by units of the armed forces and were never seen alive again. Brutal tortures of every description were used against the prisoners, whose bodies were often dumped into the ocean from military transports.

The world was horrified by even the fragmentary reports that filtered out of Argentina. When Jimmy Carter became president in 1977 and made protection of human rights a central goal of his administration, he appointed a fierce, uncompromising woman, Patt Derian, to ensure that the State Department and U.S. embassies made human rights a very high priority. I was in Guatemala at the time, and I frankly regretted the confrontational way that Derian and Carter sought to advance human rights. Many of my diplomatic colleagues shared my sentiments. I didn't support their fixation on the idea that human rights could best be protected by the U.S. publicly, unilaterally, and menacingly confronting and pressuring repressive regimes. I was convinced such a policy would have contrary results, even if it filled some Americans with satisfaction for taking a high moral stand. I felt it would be far more effective to use strong, concentrated, international pressure on these regimes, relying on diplomacy and economic leverage rather than open confrontation. Economic pressures were the most effective but difficult to employ. And after all, a cornered, unshackled lion is very dangerous. Shackling the beast was a daunting challenge, but I felt it could be done, if we took a more nuanced approach. My position cost me my post in Guatemala.

Among Raul Alfonsín's first actions as president was the creation of the National Commission on the Disappeared, headed by the noted Argentine novelist Ernesto Sabato. The Commission painstakingly investigated each of the thousands of state abductions, torture sessions, and killings. Their authoritative report, "*Nunca Más,*" issued in September 1984, makes horrifying reading, but its publication had a very positive effect in Argentina, helping bring some closure to that terrible episode in Argentine history.

I was fascinated to find in the report's appendix a case-by-case recording of the time, date, and place of the government's abduction of leftist militants, including the name of each abductee. I found it ironic that a high percentage of these killings took place in 1977–79, at the very time that President Carter and Patt Derian were pushing the policy of open U.S. confrontation with the military junta. As in Guatemala, the U.S. had very little political leverage over the Argentine junta and we and our allies avoided imposing effective economic pressures. I believe forceful economic and political pressures would have been more effective in persuading oppressive regimes that their own interests would be better served if they stopped the murdering and received foreign support. However there is no doubt that by following a policy that would involve less public confrontation, we would have demoralized those sectors suffering the repression, who looked to the U.S. for support. Most would have felt betrayed by the U.S. Nonetheless, during those dreadful years U.S. policy had only a marginal effect on the killings, as a review of the statistics clearly demonstrates.

As a result of the Sabato Commission's report, nine members of the Argentine military junta and many other lesser military leaders were brought to trial for their crimes. This was an unprecedented event, representing a break with the usual, laissez-faire response to military excess in Latin America. After the military justice system refused to try the officers, a bipartisan civilian court took on the task. I assigned an embassy officer to attend the trials as a show of support for the new government's efforts to bring about justice. I myself attended several hearings, which was favorably noted. While nothing could erase the horrors of the "dirty war," bringing justice to those most guilty brought some satisfaction and closure while also serving as a deterrent to future repressive actions.

Such was the turbulent prelude to our new mission in Buenos Aires, one of the great cities of the world. The American Ambassador's residence in Buenos Aires is on the scale of the White House in Washington, but with some lavish features. Spacious grounds, including a swimming pool, a tennis court, and formal gardens, surround the huge edifice, which is situated in the best area of Buenos Aires. The White House staff would die to have the Embassy's enormous, sweeping staircase.

We set up shop at this magnificent residence. Dolores is very efficient at this process. First, she called in the staff, which numbered about 13 individuals, and said, "Look, in this house, I don't want to hear any of you say, 'I'm the upstairs maid,' or 'I'm the chief butler,' or 'I'm the doorman.' Each of us will do what needs to be done, including my husband and I. We'll all pitch in. This is the president's house and we must always be ready to do the best we can."

The staff didn't appreciate Dolores' egalitarian approach at first, but very shortly they gelled into a team. In no time, many in official circles in Buenos Aires wanted to be invited to our place, where they knew they could count on meeting representatives of many sectors of the community. We hosted balls with good music in the elegant surroundings of the large ballroom. People dressed up and danced the tango, a dance beautiful to see and very popular in Buenos Aires. Through these social events, Dolores and I in a very short while established good personal relationships with the most influential Argentines.

One of the tricks I used to attract people, especially men, to luncheons was to pass around little shots of vodka, straight up in little cups, as a "tongue loosener." We'd all down a few shots of vodka, and it worked like a charm; everybody began to guffaw, loosen up and start talking.

Our integration into the inner official circles proceeded apace, but we did face many challenges. Just before our arrival in Buenos Aires, my friend, the favored candidate Luder, was defeated, much to everybody's surprise. Instead, a small town lawyer named Raúl Alfonsín, from the statist Radical Party, won the election. Alfonsín and his party advocated a welfare state, believing that the government had an overriding obligation to help people by providing them with entitlement programs. Alfonsín and the Radical Party harbored deep suspicions about the United States and its way of governing.

President Alfonsín appointed Dante Caputo as his foreign minister. Caputo had spent a great deal of time in France and was married to a French woman whose far-left politics he shared, along with her French superiority complex toward Americans. Within that attitude, however—and perhaps at the root of it—lay a deep annoyance at the fact that Americans seemed to succeed at just about everything, while brilliant French ideas never seemed to go anywhere. Caputo, like his wife, saw himself as a leftist intellectual, fundamentally at odds with American policies and suspicious of me. Ours was not an easy relationship.

I realized early on that President Alfonsín's lack of an understanding of economic fundamentals and basic world history prohibited him from being an effective leader of an important country like Argentina. When I met with him I had to keep the conversation focused on only one or two issues at a time. If I brought up several issues, he had trouble keeping them straight. That made meaningful discussion difficult. Although an upstanding person, very honest and patriotic—a good Argentine—Alfonsín's limited experience and intellectual capacity restricted his vision so much that he was not a successful president. Because of these obvious shortcomings—and his decision to confront the military, labor, the church, and the business community—Alfonsín was forced out of office before the completion of his term, after I already had left Argentina. His Radical Party administration fully understood political freedom but failed because of its rejection of economic freedom.

Argentina's government in general shared the public's jaundiced view of a successful, dominant United States. As a consequence, the undersecretaries and others in government were difficult to work with. Nevertheless, within a relatively short period of time, Dolores and I won acceptance across the board. The Argentines looked beyond our nationality and saw us as human beings who enjoyed each other's company and shared a vision of a stable, prosperous Argentina.

Argentine officials listened to what I had to say. I was particularly successful with the people who had the real power—the owners of the newspapers and big industries, a few labor leaders, and the intellectual elite. These power brokers had always been oriented toward Europe, but that began to change, thanks in part to a very good U.S. cultural program that included an excellent American library, the Lincoln Library, in Buenos Aires.

We began actively to encourage Argentines to go to New York, Chicago, and other important American cities. Most Argentines knew little of Chicago, for example, and had no idea what business and cultural attractions it and other American cities had to offer. Soon after we initiated the push to raise Argentine awareness of the U.S., it became "in" to know America and to travel to American cities. This represented quite a change in attitude. Within six months of arriving in Buenos Aires, we stopped hearing about the Falklands War. It seemed that all was forgiven of the U.S., even among the military leaders, who we thought would especially hate us.

A couple of fortunate circumstances in our personal lives helped us in winning the military's acceptance. My wife grew up in a military family, so she knew how to relate to the Argentine military establishment, especially the officers' wives. And my son Stephen, who was then in the 82nd Airborne Division, came to stay with us. While in Buenos Aires, he trained and jumped with the Argentine parachutists. That was unprecedented. The personal relationships that developed through these contacts greatly ameliorated the stress over Argentina's loss in the Falklands War. Although I strongly supported the U.S. policy of opposing Latin American military intervention in democratic processes, I made it my personal practice to deal with military leaders as individuals who could be reasoned with, until they proved otherwise. Then, for me, it became a search to determine what pressures or inducements could be effective to bring about reasonableness.

We found that those who had been our bitterest enemies became close acquaintances whom we could influence. For example, Argentina's top military brass maintain impressive residences at a huge military encampment in Buenos Aires, the Campo de Mayo. We were invited frequently to Campo de Mayo, which was very unusual. Few other Ambassadors enjoyed that privilege. We exercised it to our full advantage because the military had—and has always had—excessive power in Argentina. We realized we couldn't influence government actions if we didn't know the military leaders personally. We succeeded in exercising some influence over the Argentine power structure because of our access to military as well as to democratic political and labor leaders.

Apparently, the Argentine military learned well the dangers of intervening in the political processes during our time there. The military since has acquiesced to being downsized and has stayed out of politics for the past twenty years. There was a brief outbreak of military insubordination against President Alfonsín shortly after our departure. My successor Ambassador Gildred, backed strongly by President Reagan, effectively saw to it that the Argentine military stayed in their barracks. I like to think I may have helped them see the wisdom of that course. I attribute this success largely to a non-confrontational style that flew in the face of the conventional wisdom prevalent among too many of my American colleagues, who preferred to confront and ostracize the military. I think my approach worked better.

Our assignment in Buenos Aires lasted three years, 1983 to 1986. Progressively, we were able to build a relationship between the U.S. and Argentina that reached what many thought was the best it had ever been. We went from the basement to the turret in three years. Problems with the mindset of the Argentine government persisted, however. For example, the Argentine government supported the Sandinistas in Nicaragua, which we did not think was a smart move, and it was pro-Cuban. But these were minor problems in the big picture. Argentina's foreign debt—much of it to U.S. banks—posed more overwhelming challenges. In Argentina, even the provinces are authorized to receive loans from foreign banks to finance their projects, and many of them did so. This saddled Argentina with a huge foreign debt. The country's inability to make the payments on these foreign obligations led to financial havoc and political strain. American banks, because of their heavy involvement, were pressing the embassy to help them collect.

The economic troubles that Argentina faced presented me with my biggest challenges. Fortunately, the number two officer in the embassy, John Bushnell, was very capable in economic and financial fields, where I'm not so strong. He stayed on top of the situation. We wrote every week to update U.S. Treasury officials, who were keen to monitor Argentina's progress in solving the debt problem.

As we struggled to help Argentina get a grip on its finances, John Kenneth Galbraith, a well-known liberal American economist, paid a visit to the country. Galbraith was about 6'4" tall, a very impish sort of fellow, and, as a liberal Democrat, tremendously anti-Reagan. He volunteered to advise the Argentines on their foreign debt problem. The President of Argentina gave a dinner for him and invited me, which did not please Galbraith. He surmised that a Reagan appointee like me must be an avid Reaganite. He didn't trust me at all. During the dinner, I was stunned to hear Galbraith urge the Argentines to default on their loans. To back up his advice, he recalled American history. He said that during the 1870s and 80s, the states of Mississippi, Alabama, and Georgia had borrowed heavily from the British to build such infrastructure as railroads and harbors—then they decided not to pay the British back. It didn't do them any harm to default on their debts, he explained, so Argentina shouldn't worry about repercussions if it failed to pay back the money it owed international bankers. "Don't ruin yourselves just to pay back those banks," he said. "They have so much money that they won't miss it, anyway."

When Galbraith was done, Argentina's president turned to me and asked my opinion. I responded, "Well, if you follow the advice of Mr.

Galbraith and don't pay the money back, what will happen when you go back to the banks for another loan? If you're never going to ask for a loan again, do what he says. But if you ever want to borrow money again, you'd better not default." The President thought a while and then asked, "You mean the banks won't lend to us again if we don't pay them." I said, "Would you?" The President saw my point. My counsel to the Argentines enraged Galbraith.

I then suggested that the White House send down somebody with different ideas. They dispatched Paul Volker. Like Galbraith, Paul Volker was extremely tall, perhaps 6'6." Dolores had to tie two beds together to give him room to sleep at an angle. His huge shoes took half a can of my scarce American shoe polish. Volker, chairman of the Federal Reserve, had sound advice for the Argentines, suggesting that they restructure their loans. He strongly advised against defaulting, essentially repeating the caution that I had proffered earlier.

Argentina's leaders listened to Paul Volker and restructured their debt. This helped Argentina escape from its immediate financial difficulties. I felt good knowing I did a small bit to resolve a very difficult situation. (Later, in the presence of my boss, Secretary of State Shultz, President Reagan said to me, "I don't understand what your Argentine friends are up to. They are borrowing money to get out of debt." "They're buying time," I replied, "which is better for us." Both men nodded their approval.)

The high point of my service in Argentina was arranging President Alfonsín's state visit to the U.S. Because this was to be a tribute to Latin America's democratic hope, it took weeks preparing the smallest details of the itinerary. Every guest list, each seating arrangement, all the meeting times had to be worked and reworked. I was pleased with the final plan. The president would arrive in the U.S. in Williamsburg, Virginia, and spend the night there. A ceremonial reception by President Reagan on the back lawn of the White House the next day would feature cannonades, troops, music, and formal speeches. An elegant White House dinner was planned, as well as receptions and a presentation by Alfonsín to a joint session of Congress. We would then fly to New York for more of the same, and then to Chicago, Albuquerque, and Houston.

Fate, of course, intervened with our well-laid plans. The Argentine president's plane blew an engine en route to the U.S., forcing the cancellation of the elaborate Williamsburg arrival ceremonies. In Alfonsín's absence, it was our solemn duty to enjoy what taxpayers had paid for. Dolores and I, as well as members of the Protocol Office, spent that night in the greatest luxury, eating exquisite presidential meals and sleeping in ample presidential beds. We were surrounded by banks of flowers and a wait staff that catered to our every need.

When Alfonsín arrived the next day, we successfully proceeded with our itinerary. A short time before Alfonsín's speech to the joint session of Congress, we were appalled to see that well over half the congressional seats were empty. The Argentines would have been profoundly insulted by such a sight. We ran around the building, rounded up all the well-dressed tourists and capitol staff we could find, and plopped them in the empty seats. We instructed them to applaud vigorously and not to leave until Alfonsín's speech ended. The Argentines were unaware of the ruse and in fact were quite impressed by the waves of applause that greeted Alfonsín's oratory. For their part, the tourists were delighted to have such an unusual experience during their visit to the capitol.

In Chicago we ran into more minor glitches. The city's flamboyant mayor insisted that his lady friend—a large, buxom, highly painted woman—be included in all functions. She alone almost filled the presidential limousine to capacity. This presented some logistical difficulties. But these minor problems didn't diminish the success of Alfonsín's state visit. I felt that we succeeded in softening many of the Argentine's suspicions about U.S. politics and culture and giving them a first-hand view of America's success.

Alfonsín's visit to New Mexico went very well also. The president of the University of New Mexico, Dr. Farar, a highly outspoken critic of the Argentine military government's brutal war on dissidents, was a strong supporter of the Alfonsín government. Needless to say, Alfonsín was very well received by the University. A second reason for the success of the New Mexico visit was the fact that this is my home state. It pleased Alfonsín greatly that I would bring him here.

A series of health setbacks affected my service in Argentina and changed the course of my career. The ordeal began with kidney stones, which I probably developed because of the country's famously rich diet. Having kidney stones was the most painful experience I had ever endured, but, fortunately, the condition was easily cured.

Months later, a more serious problem emerged from nowhere one day as I was taking Senator Richard Lugar of Indiana to call on the vice president of Argentina in the capitol building. This impressive building, modeled after our capitol, includes a senate wing, a house wing, and a large, central dome. As we passed through the revolving door at the entrance to the building, accompanied by the chief of protocol for the Argentine Congress, my entire right side suddenly went dead. I stood stunned as my hand dropped, my foot dragged, and I was rendered incapable of speech. Oddly, nobody noticed my condition because the senator and the chief of protocol were just then shaking hands. I was standing in the background, wondering if I was going to fall over. In the next moment, the chief of protocol said, "Let's go call on the vice president," and turned around and walked off with Lugar. I made an effort to walk and by a miracle, I could do it. The paralysis had passed, but I was scared witless.

Medical specialists in Argentina failed to find any blockage in my main arteries. So I flew to the States where further tests showed a protrusion on one of the veins on the left side of my brain. Wasting no time, the physicians wheeled me into surgery, sawed my head open, jiggled the brain around and clipped the aneurysm before it had a chance to burst. Had it ruptured, I wouldn't have survived.

I awoke from the procedure to a most remarkable experience: I found myself with a new and almost frightening sense of memory. Apparently, the manipulation of my brain matter stimulated a heightened capacity for remembering. I had total recall, to the point where I could with little effort smell, touch, see, feel, things that happened at my fifth birthday party, for example. This amazing capacity persisted for quite some time—to this day, in fact, although it has diminished since the first years after the operation.

I returned to Argentina with a shaved head. In order to continue with my normal, very public activities, I decided to wear a *boina* (beret). I had to choose my color carefully, however, because in Argentina, the color of a boina identifies one's political affiliation. I decided to wear a black one, which had no particular political connotation, to stay out of trouble. People made fun of me for that, but they were very supportive.

I was besieged with still more health problems in Argentina, and these demanded lengthy treatment in the U.S. I asked for an assignment to the University of New Mexico in Albuquerque as a Diplomat in Residence. This would allow me to obtain treatment at the Lovelace Clinic and also put me in a position to retire in Santa Fe, as I had always planned to do.

Just as my tour in Buenos Aires was concluding, I became embroiled in a classic Washington political blood fest that again put me on the front pages of newspapers. It began when a political activist in the State Department leaked to the press a highly classified report that I had sent to the U.S. Secretary of State and the President. The report concerned the visit to Argentina of a congressional delegation headed by the Speaker of the House, Tip O'Neill. My report, classified NODIS (no distribution) and under strict control, was supposed to be read only by very few top officials. I classified the report NODIS because I had been instructed to make a frank appraisal of the speaker's attempt to counter President Reagan's policies in Central America, especially in Nicaragua.

In Washington, all but open warfare raged over the president's strong support of the Contra rebellion against the Sandinista government in Nicaragua. Speaker O'Neill personally expressed outrage at the murder of Catholic priests and nuns at the hands of the anti-Marxists in Central America. Some of the brutally murdered religious were either related to or known to O'Neill. The Congress had passed legislation intended to stop U.S. support for the anti-Marxist groups, especially the Contras in Nicaragua. The administration, however, was determined to continue its hard-line policies against the Marxists. The political struggle was savage.

O'Neill and the Democratic congressmen in his group expected to use their visit to whip up Latin American support for congressional opposition to the President's Central American policies. The precept that "politics stop at the ocean's edge," a laudable tradition in American politics, unfortunately had long since died. Argentina, under the leadership of Foreign Minister Caputo, had already made generous loans to Castro's Cuba and to the Sandinista government in Nicaragua. The speaker felt sure he could persuade the Argentine government to side publicly with the Democrats and defy President Reagan. The Argentines had that predisposition, and a strong public position by the Argentine government against Reagan's policies would be quite a blow to the U.S. administration. Mexico had already taken such a position. As the American Ambassador to Argentina, I was caught in the middle.

O'Neill's visit started off fine. My custom of serving small but potent shots of vodka at the beginning of meetings to loosen tongues soon had O'Neill and Dolores (whose maternal grandfather was an O'Neill) singing "When Irish Eyes are Smiling," with the whole delegation joining in.

The levity was gone during meetings with the Argentines the next day. O'Neill had brought the American press with him to report, he hoped, on the Latin opposition to President Reagan. When we were escorted into President Alfonsín's conference room, I was disturbed to see American newsmen brazenly marching in and taking seats at the table. I insisted to President Alfonsín that they be asked to leave and he agreed. Among those expelled from the conference room was Representative Russo of Chicago, who brazenly had planned to film and tape the entire meeting on his camcorder. I allowed him back in the room without his machine. It occurred to me that policing Alfonsín's office was not my job, but I felt compelled to do so because the Argentines couldn't tell the difference between American newsmen and congressmen.

The meeting was a love fest, but the canny Argentine president avoided openly attacking President Reagan, no matter how hard O'Neill tried to get him to do so. There was no doubt, however, that Alfonsín and Caputo were with O'Neill.

The meetings with the Argentine congressmen and Senators were another matter. Some made wild, accusatory, damning comments against Reagan's policies, although others, especially those in leadership positions, offered balanced comments, many in support of U.S. policy. When I tried to end the meeting because we were late for a luncheon, an Argentine senator yelled at me, accusing me of trying to stop the attacks on U.S. policy.

O'Neill's visit was a huge headache for me, and I was relieved when he and his entourage took their leave. O'Neill's Irish eyes were not so smiley when I saw him off at the airport, but he was polite with me and effusive with Dolores. Afterwards, I submitted what I considered to be an accurate, balanced report on the visit to the President and the Secretary of State, although I did not report Congressman Russo's idiotic behavior. Believing the NODIS channel to be absolutely secure, I was candid in my report, as I generally am.

I was stunned in a couple of days when the wire services and reporters began hounding me. Someone had given my entire report to the media, and they loved it. It detailed O'Neill's shenanigans as he tried his hardest to discredit Reagan. The news stories claimed I was "appalled" by O'Neill's actions, described the Argentines as taking sides, and went on and on with a description of O'Neill's visit.

O'Neill called a press conference in Washington to attack me for showing a lack of respect for Congress. (Interestingly, he made it a point to praise Dolores.) All this was grist for the media mill. I decided to keep mum and let the State Department do the talking. The first announcement the Department made was of the firing of the officer who leaked my report. The Department described my report as a personal, confidential missive to the Secretary of State that was not intended as a criticism of Congress. By keeping mum, I did not fan the fires of the outcry. Only when a nasty Argentine press story claimed that I had engineered the whole affair did I make a public denial. Soon thereafter O'Neill left the Congress and I left Buenos Aires.

A 1990 Argentine history book of the period (Sola's *Asalto a la Ilusion)* states that I was removed [sic] from my post "for having injured the political dignity" of a "respected old-timer" who "enjoyed the protection of the Kennedy family and could not be mistreated by an Ambassador."

This was not the way I wanted to be remembered in Argentina, and happily, that was not the case. Our mission there was probably one of the most successful in my career. I had firm instructions from President Reagan for my assignment to Argentina. There were as follows in order of priority:

1. Institutionalization of democracy;
2. Implementation of more market and private sector-orientated economic policies and responsible management of trade and investment policies and the foreign debt;
3. Increase in safeguards and other nuclear nonproliferation actions;
4. Continuation of Argentine orientation toward peaceful solutions for Falklands' tensions and a constructive and moderating role in Hemsipheric and world affairs;
5. Enhancement of our military-to-military relationships while promoting the Argentine military's respect for civilian control and democratic principles; and
6. Increased effectiveness of Argentina's anti-drug activities and assumption of a constructive leadership role in Hemispheric action against the drug menance.

My Embassy was able to achieve those goals to a large degree. On our departure we received numerous demonstrations of personal affection from Argentine colleagues, who showered us with tributes. We were very happy in Argentina and maintain contact with good friends there.

As I left Argentina, my last overseas posting, I reflected on over 30 years of service in the Western Hemisphere. I felt great pride in knowing that by 1990, for the first time in history, all Latin American countries except for Cuba were governed by democratically elected leaders. This was an insistant goal of President Reagan. I knew I had contributed to some small degree in creating that hope-inspiring situation. The diplomatic service bestows an abundance of psychological rewards if scant material ones.

Rear gardens of our residence in Buenos Aires, Argentina, with pet

Embassy staff on the Grand Staircase,
American Embassy, Buenos Aires, Argentina, 1985

Receiving Honorary Degree, University of New Mexico 1986

My wonderful family: Cristina Elisa, James Thomas, Stephen Hernan, Frank Vincent de Paul, and Dolores, 1978

Cuddling the last grandchild, Lucas Ortiz

16

Home at Last—But Not for Long

The State Department granted my request for an assignment to New Mexico for medical treatments. Soon after arriving, I took up my duties as an adjunct professor at the University of New Mexico in the Political Science Department. My full title was Diplomat in Residence, which initially made me something of a campus oddity.

In 1986 the University had granted me an honorary doctorate, but I felt less than honored as I returned to the campus. I soon found out that carrying out my assignment at UNM would not be easy. Many faculty colleagues were products of the raging 1960s. They tended to regard any U.S. government official as an agent for all that is "evil, brutal, corrupt, mendacious, stupid and dangerous," as I reported to the State Department about my position at the University.

Some university groups seemed to perceive me as an envoy from hell, especially those on the liberal left, who were firmly entrenched and highly vocal about their abhorrence of their own government's policies, leadership, and actions. Unsurprisingly, they held views that were charitable to a notable degree when it came to the policies, leaders, and actions of the authoritarian, leftist governments that the U.S. government, in assuring common interests, sought to contain or oppose. To these more extreme elements, someone like me—a high-level U.S. government official who undeniably had dealt with corrupt, right-wing dictators—was a clear and present danger.

Seldom was I subjected to open hostility, but I frequently encountered sullenness and generally was excluded from campus events. There were exceptions, of course. The chair of the Political Science Department, Dr. Paul Hain, was always attentive and interested in my work. He set me up in a fine office, after the Latin American Studies department, my logical home, banished me to a remote cell. The ever-effervescent Fred Harris—who knew enough about the American political system to make a run for the presidency, which he did—was unfailingly friendly and supportive. Gradually, most students and faculty came to accept me as a professor who was just different from the academic mainstream, and not necessarily evil, even if I remained a potential corruptor of young minds.

My unique position as Diplomat in Residence came with some privileges. I could select my students, for example, and I could limit my class size to 30 students. I also chose to accept only juniors or seniors. This allowed me to put together good classes on American foreign policy and American diplomatic history. My schedule was not grueling. We lived in Santa Fe and I traveled to the University in Albuquerque only two days a week. I suspect that my less than overwhelming presence on campus was a comfort to those who perceived me as a menace to their hegemony.

I gleaned much of value from the experience at UNM. I learned a lot about the younger generation of Americans—and not all of it was good. Most dramatically, I was shocked at evidence of the shortcomings of the American educational system. My students were among the cream of the crop, and, on the whole, they were intelligent. But many of them wrote poorly. They couldn't spell. Their lack of English skills I found unsettling. I preferred essay questions in the tests I gave them, so I could see how well the students expressed themselves. Often their answers were nearly unintelligible. In order to grade fairly, I'd also include absolute, true-or-false or one-answer questions; their responses to these also often shocked me. In response to the test question, "In what city is the headquarters of the United Nations?"

one of my best students answered, "In Cicili [sic]." Flabbergasted, I called the student in and asked what he meant by his answer. "Isn't it in Sicily?" he replied. This from one of my best students! That marked a low point in my teaching experience.

I devised a rather novel way of teaching, giving my students exercises to simulate real-world situations. I assigned each student to represent a particular pressure group—the agricultural lobby, the banking lobby, the Jewish lobby, the Greek lobby, and so on. I told them that their government most often responded to strong pressures from these special interests. Then I presented them with a situation and asked, "How would your government react to this?" Each student had to support his or her group's viewpoint. The exercises proved very useful in demonstrating to students the complexities that influenced government policies. The fun of this kind of hands-on, group oriented exercise made my classes very popular. By my second year, students were anxious to get into my classes. When students rated their professors at the end of the school year, I came out very well. That pleased me.

I made my share of mistakes while at UNM. For example, the situation in Nicaragua was at the time a topic of heated discussion on campus. I was invited to give a talk on U.S. policies toward Nicaragua. I faced a very hostile audience and further stirred the hornets' nest by acting the smart aleck. When one of the students stood up and yelled, "We're killing babies! We're killing babies!" referring to our actions in Nicaragua, I sarcastically said, "Let's keep the abortion fight out of this." That was a mistake.

In spite of the minor difficulties, Dolores and I enjoyed a break from the normal diplomatic routine during my time at UNM. We didn't miss bodyguards and the endless daily demands on our time. We weren't required to go out every night for two or three diplomatic engagements. It was OK to turn down dinner invitations! For forty years I had sublimated my own needs, thoughts, and desires, doing what duty demanded, whether I wanted to do it or not. We had grown accustomed to all manner of aggravations—horrible meals, terrible hours, awful people, suspicious, baseless accusations—but at UNM, for the first time in my professional life, I could more or less do what I wanted and say what I felt. It was a liberating and refreshing experience.

In Santa Fe, Dolores and I began our long-awaited adjustment to being home. I began to become active in local community organizations—a habit that would expand greatly later, when I returned to Santa Fe for good. Through the efforts of an extraordinary civic leader, Susan Herter, I became a trustee of the Museum of New Mexico Foundation—a position of great importance to me. Susan is a sort of civic midwife who has helped give birth to many constructive civic organizations. She also introduced me to the North American Institute, a remarkably effective but little-known organization headquartered in Santa Fe that worked to bring Canada, the United States, and Mexico into a closer union. The Institute had many successes, culminating in 2000 with a tripartite meeting in Santa Fe of the foreign ministers of the three countries.

After two very successful years at UNM, my medical problem was under control and the State Department called me back to Washington on assignment. I don't recall any fervently warm wishes or expressions of regret from most of the faculty at UNM upon our departure. I find it gratifying, however, that students with whom I bonded still stay in contact with me.

It had occurred to State Department officials that since I'd had experience in many embassies (I was head of mission five times), that I was just the person to help oversee a restructuring of the State Department. This did not come as good news to me, since the task could involve, in effect, vexing or downgrading friends. It would be my responsibility to negotiate contracts with companies to critically examine State Department operations and recommend expense cutbacks and generally how best to redirect the department's efforts.

I was not terribly happy with this assignment, which didn't draw on my particular skills and talents. It's not the type of thing I'm best at. My job would put me in the unenviable position of making employees explain, in quantifiable terms, just what it was they were doing. We'd have to ask them to justify their activities, explain why they were necessary, and devise ways to perform their duties more effectively—or comment on whether their positions should be abolished. I was not wildly successful at this unpleasant task, which was made worse because many I worked with shirked the tough, confrontational work. Many bailed out, more or less, leaving me with the responsibility. After a while I recognized that it was a good time for me to bail, too. I had reached retirement age and Dolores agreed: it was a good time to retire from the Service.

I announced my retirement and as we readied ourselves to leave Washington for good, I was surprised by an invitation from the Soviet government to visit Russia. The invitation, which came through the Novosti News Agency, included about thirty American leaders. I thought an official trip to the USSR—a world unknown to me—would make a wonderful ending to my career.

Our contingent flew to Helsinki and then to Moscow in April 1990, where we received a red carpet treatment. President Gorbachev's office and his wife Raisa treated us very well. The USSR was in a state of great excitement and turmoil, as Gorbachev's policy of openness to the West was bringing many changes to the country, not all of them welcome. The Gorbachevs, while popular among progressive, pro-Western factions, faced strong opposition from those who were against giving up the old ways. This was vividly demonstrated one night when we were invited to a theater for a performance created especially for us. Gorbachev could not attend, but his wife was to be our hostess. When we arrived at the theater, we were perplexed to see that Raisa's box was empty. She waited to take her seat until the lights went out, fearing the jeers that would have accompanied her arrival in a lighted theater. She also left before the lights went on. That was a real eye-opener for me, to see how unpopular the Gorbachevs were in their own country.

The Russia trip was instructive for me in other ways as well. For years the American media had focused on the power and greatness of the Soviet Union and the tremendous threat it posed to the U.S. Once there, I was astonished at the miserable condition of the country. As we drove around Moscow, we saw lines of people at stores. Any time a shipment of shoes, oranges, pants—whatever—came in, the word would go around and droves of people would line up to buy the items. The lack of almost everything shocked me. I wasn't prepared for it. I felt betrayed by the American media and unhappy with the journalists who had failed to portray the Soviet Union in a more realistic light.

I avoided official guides in the USSR. Instead I went to the University of Moscow to hire a young fellow who spoke English. I asked him to accompany me on excursions around town. When I told my guide of my shock at the depressed state of his country and asked about the people standing in lines, he said simply, "We have nothing." I wanted to understand this for myself, so I suggested that we undertake a little experiment.

I asked my guide how many people there were in his family. He counted off his sister, mother, father and grandmother—five people living together. I offered to treat the family to a nice dinner that night. I said we'd go shopping for the foods the family liked best. They would prepare and consume the meal at their home. "That's going to be very difficult," he cautioned me. I responded that I wanted to know just how difficult it would be.

We planned to have chicken for dinner, since chicken seemed generally to be available. We took our place in a long line at the place that sold chickens. We shuffled along slowly for about 45 minutes to reach a poultry case piled with scrawny, sad looking chickens, their feet, heads, and wing feathers still intact, but their flesh badly bruised. They were in terrible shape! Such chicken could never be sold in the U.S. I pointed to two of the least damaged carcasses and the saleswoman removed them from the case, wrapped them in paper, and then gave me a note. We took the note to another line, where we stood again for about half an hour, waiting to pay for the two chickens. Once I handed over a few rubles, I received another piece of paper, this one stamped, to show that I'd paid. Then we went to stand in another line, where I presented the stamped note and received the chickens.

We had in our possession two chickens after almost one and a half tedious hours. So then I said, "How about some potatoes?" Alas, there were no potatoes to be had anywhere—but we did find turnips and a variety of long cucumbers. We endured the same dreary procedure to buy them, standing in one line to pay for them, and others to actually obtain them. Next we embarked on a search for bread. Supplies of good, white breads had run out, so we bought coarse black bread. I thought fruit would go well with our meal, which was growing more pitiful by the moment. We drove around the city on a quest for apples. In that sprawling city of five million people, we could find no apples, nor any other kind of fruit. "This isn't going to be much of a dinner," I thought to myself, But my guide, accustomed to working the system, came up with a suggestion: we could go to the university where a friend of his worked in the faculty kitchen. "For a little bribe we can get some sausages," my guide said. I said, "Okay. Let's do it."

Off we went to the University, where my guide entered shamelessly through the kitchen's back door. He made the deal: $20 for three sausages. Now, after almost an entire day of "shopping" (it was more like foraging), the ingredients for our dinner were as complete as they were going to get: two scrawny chickens, four cucumbers, a few turnips, three sausages, and some black bread.

It wasn't just food that was in short supply in the Soviet Union in those days. Often Russians you met would ask, "Before you leave, could I buy your jeans? Could I buy your shirt?" That's how awful conditions were—they'd buy the clothes right off your back. Needless to say, people were extremely unhappy with the situation, and they blamed Gorbachev. The nationwide scarcity of goods was one of the main reasons for his unpopularity.

Still, the Russians managed to keep a sense of humor. While standing in the chicken line, my guide translated some jokes going around. He told one about a man who was in a long line, waiting to buy shoes. This fellow declared he was fed up with waiting and he was going to go shoot Gorbachev. Off he went, only to return in an hour to the line, which hadn't moved very far. The people around him asked, "Well, why did you come back? Did you shoot Gorbachev?" And he replied, "No, that line is longer than this one!"

To my knowledge, there is not even an itinerant drop of Russian blood in the family, and it came as a surprise and a revelation when I felt very much at home there. This first struck me at Zagorsk, a small village outside Moscow. Pilgrims trek regularly to the monastery there. As luck would have it, I arrived in Zagorsk on Good Friday in the Orthodox calendar. Hundreds of people were walking from all parts of the country, some carrying crosses, just like some do in New Mexico as they walk to the *Santuario* in Chimayó. I was moved to see faces so like those at the Santuario on Good Friday, filled with devotion and deep, abiding faith.

I presented the High Priest in Zagorsk with a box of American chocolates and he went berserk with pleasure. After that, I received the VIP tour of the monastery. I then traveled by train to St. Petersburg, then called Leningrad, for Easter. The enthusiasm for religious ceremonies there was even more fervent. Gorbachev, as part of his policy of glasnost, had just liberalized policies relating to religion. People packed all the churches, to the point that it was almost dangerous to enter a church. The congregations were composed mostly of young people expressing a great outburst of long-suppressed religious fervor. For anyone from our region, it was easy to understand their devotion, which reminded me so much of observances among New Mexico's faithful.

My trip to the USSR was the capstone of my professional career. After I returned, I retired from the Foreign Service with the usual ceremony. The State Department presented me with an American flag and there were speeches about how wonderful it had been to have me in the Service. The appreciation was welcome, but it didn't compare to the satisfaction I felt personally. I knew I had made a difference and no one could ever take that from me. It wouldn't have mattered if nobody knew of or appreciated my contributions. I knew at the end of my career that I had accomplished much of what I set out to do in the Service. Accolades aside, that remains the primary reward of a professional life.

17

Home to Stay: More Lessons to Learn

After the trip to the USSR, we began our move to New Mexico for the final time. We always knew Santa Fe would be our final destination, so we put our house in Washington up for sale. Although comparable in price with others on the market, our house languished for several months without a sale. Dolores recalled a tradition among the devout of burying an image of St. Joseph in the yard to induce a sale. My only comment was, "Whatever you do, don't let anybody know you did such a silly thing!" To my astonishment, no sooner had St. Joseph taken up residence in the back garden than the house sold at what was to us an astonishing price. (An image of St. Joseph now greets guests from over the entrance to our new house.)

We had paid $39,000 for the Washington house and had rented it for many years to pay the kids' tuition bills. By the time we sold it, it had appreciated dramatically and we realized a handsome profit. The tax laws allowed us to invest the money in another principal residence. The upshot was that we were able to build our dream house in Santa Fe using the gains we made on our modest initial investment.

In June 1990, Dolores and I returned to Santa Fe. After nearly 40 years of moving from one end of the world to the other, we finally came home to roost. It was a wonderful feeling. And now that we've been here 14 years, I realize that my time in New Mexico has exceeded by far our stay at any of my foreign service posts, including Washington, D.C.

In Santa Fe we rented a temporary house while we began building our dream house. We had been imagining this house for decades, collecting various items from all the countries where we lived with which to embellish it. I had a floor plan handy so over the years I made revisions that occurred to me.

I took great care with the final construction plans. The house plan works very well; our home gracefully handles heavy use. An English magazine featured it as an American style that Europeans should know about. Maybe I missed my calling. I think I'd make a good architect.

I found that my perspective on Santa Fe and the United States had changed somewhat after decades overseas. In my absence, Santa Fe had become a very sophisticated town. World-class, creative people call Santa Fe home. It had always attracted interesting people, but in recent years there has been a quantum leap. We certainly didn't feel we were returning to an intellectual or cultural backwater.

I wanted to be active during my retirement in Santa Fe. I had many projects in mind, and knew that the skill I learned in my various postings could prove useful. Even before our return I began to focus on a problem of great concern to me: the situation at the Palace of the Governors history museum. In previous visits to the museum, which is the repository of New Mexico's historic patrimony, I asked to be shown the collections because I knew they contained remarkable artifacts, some of which my family had donated. I understood that the old building lacked the space to exhibit them all, but assumed the artifacts were in safe storage somewhere. But I wanted to be sure.

When I was shown the dank basements and fire-prone bays where collections were stored, I was horrified and outraged. In fact, I flew into a monumental rage. The conditions were absolutely shocking—so bad that the historic patrimony of New Mexico, our New Mexico, could have vanished in a flash. Overhead dangled loose electrical wires whose purpose nobody knew, alongside steam pipes that could have burst at any time, ruining countless artifacts. Sewer back-ups, heavy rain, and feckless toilets had all caused flooding. I found the situation not only incredible, but also totally unacceptable. It was not difficult to find others who shared my indignation. We formed a group called *Los Compadres del Palacio,* Friends of the Palace, to urgently remedy this appalling situation.

The calamitous conditions at the state's history museum had existed for at least 50 years, but the imminent threat of losing thousands of irreplaceable artifacts constituting the core of New Mexico's historic patrimony appeared to cause little public concern. It seemed that Santa Fe's numerous historic preservationists—official, organizational, and individual—had more important goals. After their success in saving a gas station on the corner of the historic plaza, they were focusing their energies on another funky 1930s gas station on the corner of Washington Avenue and Marcy Street. Militantly, they obliged the First State Bank to renovate this absurd relic rather than construct a new building for the bank's downtown office. All involved in this effort were obviously unaware that in a previous century this property was the site of the Palace Hotel, Santa Fe's grandest building. The bank could have justifiably razed the gas station and constructed a larger building more appropriate for the center of a royal capital and cathedral city that once administered a vast portion of a colonial empire. Finding the responsible preservationists more concerned with saving the "treasures" of the 1930s than with those irreplaceable ones of the preceding 300 years, the Compadres decided to form our own preservationist action group.

The first meeting of the Compadres took place at the home of Anita Gonzales Thomas, a wonderful civic leader, beloved by all. The historian Mary J. Shaw Cook joined the group, as did Jerry Richardson, a young lawyer with the state government. Dr. Tom Chávez, director of the history museum, assumed leadership of this small but dynamic group. Dr. Chávez was a puckish leader who proved over and over again what dedication combined with a sense of humor can accomplish. The Compadres made a great team.

The Compadres emphatically agreed to go to any lengths to save the state's historic patrimony, and we meant it. Our first challenge was immediately to find safe storage for the half million historic photographs included in the museum's photographic archives, as well as several thousand books, maps (one of the finest old map collections in the country), and historic documents. All these were stored under leaky roofs, in dusty, dangerous conditions where mice ran rampant.

About that time, the city was preparing to abandon the old city library, adjacent to the Palace of the Governors. The old library would make a perfect place for a history library and photo archive. When I inquired about the possibility, however, the mayor told me we were too late. The city had already decided that the old library would go to a real estate partnership that owned thousands of acres south of the city. The development partners planned to convert the library building into a commercial gallery. They had struck a deal with the city whereby they would transfer several acres of their land to the National Guard in exchange for the old library. The city would then assume ownership of the old National Guard headquarters and armory.

When the mayor informed Jim Snead, the head of the Museum Foundation, and me that the deal was already done, we replied, "Sir, you do not understand. You cannot do that. Your plan is not acceptable. We have to protect New Mexico's patrimony, which is now in great danger. The only place we can save many precious items is the old city library. So you're going to have to change your plans."

The mayor flew into a snit, yelling at us, "Who the hell do you think you are? You represent nobody." "OK, Mr. Mayor," I said. "It's very easy. Let's just go public with this. Let's call in the press and tell them what we want to do and what you've decided. And we'll let the public decide."

The very next day—the press clippings, which I cherish, are on file—the mayor ran up the white flag. The development partnership came out a bit unhappy because the city ended up with the National Guard properties, the National Guard acquired the land they wanted—but the partnership lost its chance at acquiring prized downtown property. The mayor was very, very annoyed with me, but remained a good friend nevertheless.

The first hurdle with state funds was behind us, but once we took possession of the old library, we were shocked at the mess it was in.

Leaks and other problems needed to be fixed before the building would be of any use. We began a campaign to raise money for renovation. It was a struggle but with more state help and private fund raising we eventually amassed enough money to restore the building and establish the Fray Angélico Chávez History Library and Photographic Archives. We held a big celebration when we moved in, feeling that we had accomplished something significant for all New Mexicans. The new library, a state-of-the-art facility, holds books, documents, maps, and now almost 800,000 historic photographs in an impeccable environment, safeguarded for the long term by sophisticated protections. (My papers and photographs are archived there.)

In the flush of victory, we felt that nothing could stop us. Considering our success as just a first step, in our plans for the museum, we took aim at our next objective: acquiring the fabulous and unique Segesser Hide paintings, which were held in a private collection in Switzerland. With the help of Senator Les Houston, the minority leader of the Senate, we obtained money through the legislature to buy the paintings. Acquiring these major Spanish Colonial relics was of more than local importance. First Lady Hillary Clinton came to Santa Fe in person to proclaim both the Palace of the Governors and the Segesser Hide paintings national treasures of the United States. Very few museums or even cities can claim those distinctions.

On a roll now, we pursued our next prize: purchase of an empty lot behind the history library for a museum annex to the Palace of the Governors. The land belonged to a family that owned commercial properties in Santa Fe, including one of the most prominent and successful contemporary art galleries. We realized that having this property was absolutely vital to realizing our dream of building a new museum. The owners, however, had already declared it would be the site for a new gallery, for which their plans were in progress. Undaunted, we made it clear that we would have to acquire that land.

We knew the history museum could never expand without that property. In fact, the land had once been part of the Palace of the Governors compound. The Palace, which used to cover almost four times the area it does now, had consistently lost land over the centuries.

Bit by bit, it was frittered away. So we held to our simple but firm resolve. We told the owners we would raise money to pay them the appraised value of the land. But they dug in their heels and insisted they would not sell. It came down to a heated confrontation, to the point that the owner refused to see me. He abhorred the sight of me.

We believed our only hope was to go into a full-court press: we decided to take the property through the process of condemnation. We knew we were on solid legal ground, because we were advised by the Museum Foundation's Jim Snead, who is an outstanding lawyer. We anticipated a counter suit from the owners, but we didn't foresee the strongly negative editorial that appeared in the *New Mexican*. Stating that condemnation would not be the "Santa Fe way" to settle the matter, the editorial opined that taking private property was not right. I penned a sharp rebuttal, pointing out that this wasn't just any old property; it was unique and invaluable, and the *New Mexican* should be supporting its acquisition by the state.

Discussion of litigation began to bother people on both sides of the issue. One of the museum regents declared her opposition to taking private property for public use—a very damaging statement coming from someone in her position. At that point, I decided the gloves would have to come off. Recognizing that it was going to be a tough fight—especially when the owners of the land began to make public statements to the effect that what we were trying to do was illegal and un-American—I contacted some retired New Mexico Supreme Court justices and asked if they would agree to picket the landowner's art gallery with me. The justices agreed.

Word of my scheme got back to the landowners and to a friend of theirs, a civic leader from New York, Chuck Diker, who had a home in Santa Fe. He and his wife loved Santa Fe and understood the significance of what we were trying to do. Diker called the landowner from New York to advise him there was no way he could win. He pointed out that pressures were building, the legal contest could go on forever, and even if the landowner won and kept the land, he would have lost on many other fronts. We offered the owner the appraised value of the land. Diker told the owner he'd be well advised to take that.

The owner finally agreed—or was forced to agree. He hasn't spoken to me since. It was a major victory for the Compadres and the museum, but we still needed to raise the money for the purchase. We obtained some money from the State Legislature and, after pointing out to the City Council that we were proposing to save a good part of the soul of downtown Santa Fe, they agreed to contribute also—but only if we provided public restrooms in the new building. We acquiesced, provided the city would police and clean the restrooms. The Museum Foundation came through with the final amount we needed, in the form of a no-strings-attached grant.

Lo and behold, after hundreds of years of giving up land, the historic Palace of the Governors gained back vital space. Now it was time to start planning the new museum annex building itself. This required that we again turn to the legislature for money to begin drawing plans. Unfortunately, not all that money we received went for our museum plans. Slices of the funds were diverted for one thing or another, which sometimes happens with state appropriations. But the state's commitment made the building a virtual certainty at some point. Finally, we could begin to look forward to having a museum worthy of our historic patrimony.

Once the initial plans were done, the new museum's estimated cost came to $23 to 25 million dollars. The longer we waited to begin building, the more the cost would rise. Raising this kind of money was extremely daunting for our group. We had faced raising a million here, $2 million there, but $25 million seemed impossible. We had to turn to the federal government. I began flying to Washington D.C. regularly, making a royal pest of myself visiting Representatives Richardson and Redmond, then Udall and Skeen (who sat on the Appropriations Committee), and Senators Bingaman and Domenici. I also made the rounds of the Hispanic Caucus. I pulled every stunt I could think of to get federal money.

Senator Domenici was the one most responsible for making our dream a reality. Our success with him unfolded in a telling way. I'd stalked him, camped in his office—every time I went to Washington I bothered him. He consistently reminded me it was difficult to get federal money for local capital improvements and that a state museum was something the state should take care of. But I pointed out that we were talking about a national monument, older than Plymouth Plantation, Independence Hall or the White House. "All those Johnny-come-latelies don't compare to the Palace of the Governors," I told him. "Next time you visit Santa Fe, let us show you." He promised us a half hour of his time during his next visit—and he made good on that commitment. He came to the museum, but, fascinated, stayed for three hours. At the end of his visit, he was as convinced as we were that saving this key element of our nation's patrimony was necessary and urgent.

Mainly through Senator Dominici's help, but with the support of many others, we were granted a hearing before the appropriate Senate committee in Washington. Tom Chávez and I flew there with some of New Mexico's treasures from the museum collections. Tom made me carry them on my lap all the way. We testified before the committee and made our case: we needed $15 million in federal funds, which we'd try to match with state funds. Things seemed to be going smoothly, but then much to our dismay, the National Park Service at the last minute testified against us. Park Service representatives insisted the money requested would have to come out of their appropriations and that they also had buildings in trouble all around the country. Fortunately, Senator Bingaman, who was also on the committee, quashed the Park Service's arguments, and the vote was unanimously in our favor, as was the vote in the House of Representatives. Presidents Clinton and Bush signed bills giving us $15 million. (Appropriately, the new building will be named for Senator Dominici.)

We then faced the difficulty of raising $15 million in matching state funds. We went into attack mode again, making nuisances of ourselves in the State Capitol roundhouse. I came to know the strengths and vanities of most state legislators as we worked ourselves to a frazzle. After a couple of years, the wise guys in the roundhouse decided to avoid taking a stand on the issue by putting the question of funding for the new museum to a vote in a statewide bond issue. Surely the voters would give us the money, since they all loved us and our plans—or so the lawmakers assured us. We were innocent enough to believe it.

As it turned out, our bond initiative was written in tiny print and buried in the middle of an election sheet that included a hodgepodge of initiatives. Nobody—not even our supporters—could find our bond to vote for it! On top of that, it snowed on election day, which dampened the general turnout. Our supporters were out in force, carrying big signs urging people to vote for Bond Issue E, for the Palace of the Governors.

We were set for our victory party as the election returns came in. Our group gathered at the Palace of the Governors, with champagne chilling, and turned on the television for what we were sure would be a great victory. We were absolutely crushed when our bond failed to win passage in one single county in the whole state—but we didn't give up. We presented ourselves again at the next legislative session, lobbying hard for a direct appropriation. With the unstinting leadership of Representative Luciano "Lucky" Varela and Senator Ben Altamirano, among others, this time the legislature appropriated a good portion of the money needed. Then, of course, Governor Johnson vetoed it, plunging us again into despair.

We regrouped and went at it again with a new approach at the next legislative session. This time the legislature passed and Governor Johnson signed a bill giving us $11 million. At that point, we knew there was no turning back and that we were going to succeed for sure. We pressed on to complete the fundraising. In 2003 Governor Richardson signed a bill appropriating another $5 million, bringing our total funding to $31 million—$16 million in state funds and $15 million in federal funds. The Office of Cultural Affairs, however, had designated almost $4 million of these funds to a statewide services building for the Museum of New Mexico. That unrelated project was tacked on to our appropriation. Then, nearly a million more dollars were drained away for archeological studies, which nearly gave me a stroke. And so it went—a little money here, a little money there, and we were down to $23 million for our building, the cost of which relentlessly increased with the passage of time. This forced us to modify our plans, removing two entire floors off the structure. We pared the building down from five stories to three. In 2004, through Governor Richardson's goodwill, we finally obtained the remaining $3 million needed for construction.

The project at the Palace of the Governors took 17 years of my life. Our group worked very hard to see the project through. Now, in spite of the disappointment at the downsizing of our plans, we celebrate the fact that we've accomplished the most important thing: New Mexico will have a museum worthy of its history.

Throughout the course of the Palace project and ever since we returned to New Mexico, I have been saddened by what I perceived to be a steady ebbing of a very precious and central part of New Mexican history and culture—the Hispanic component. It seems to be slipping away even in my own extended family. Almost none of my many nieces, nephews, or cousins speaks Spanish. But what's worse, very few of them have the vaguest idea about the significance of the Hispanic contribution to New Mexico.

My concern with that loss prompted me to join Hispanic-oriented groups. One that I care for especially is *Rancho de las Golondrinas,* a living history museum in La Cienega. I became a trustee of the Paloheimo Trust, which manages the rancho, and held office on the board. There has been remarkable growth at the rancho. We've accomplished extraordinary things—a new, big orientation center, *plazuelas* for the artisans, and a kitchen large enough to feed the 50,000 people that visit the rancho each year. Change and growth are continuing at Rancho de las Golondrinas, and joining the efforts of this outstanding organization has been a real joy.

I also became involved with the creation of the National Hispanic Cultural Center in Albuquerque, and the North American Institute. I support the Spanish Colonial Arts Society and Cornerstones, two excellent organizations. I became a member of the board of an action-oriented think tank called Think New Mexico. I've done my bit for that excellent, bipartisan organization, lobbying the legislature for full-day kindergarten, reform of the school system, for abolishment of the tax on food and medicines, and for dealing with the state's serious water problem. As a member of the Art in Public Places Committee of the City, I'm proud to have been closely involved with the creation of the statue of Santa Fe's founder, Pedro de Peralta, the Cathedral Park renovation, and the Santa Fe Trail monument. All these intense efforts have occupied and brought me great rewards during my "retirement."

Something quite different from anything I've ever experienced before has also kept me enthused and committed. My wife pulled me into this one kicking and resisting when one day she said to me, "We're going to see some kids dance—not just any kids but children from low income areas, many with problems. The dancing helps them become better children." I said to her, "Dear, you go and come back and tell me about it. I do not want to see children dancing." But Dolores was firm. She said, "You are going to watch these children dance."

The performance brought tears to my eyes. I never imagined what dance "instruction" could accomplish. I witnessed even clunky kids, perfectly disciplined, working together and achieving wonders. I was dumbfounded and before I knew it I was an officer of the National Dance Institute of New Mexico and deeply involved in trying to extend its programs. The organization has been breathtaking in its success, and working with it has been a remarkable and especially worthwhile experience

The Institute was founded by Jacques d'Amboise, one of the lead dancers of the New York City Ballet—a terrific, saintly guy. In New Mexico the Institute's co-founder, unstoppable energizer, and artistic director, Catherine Oppenheimer, is, in all senses, like an angel descended from heaven. (However, I have no idea if she has a belly button!) Others involved with the NDI board and staff were like me, hooked on a wonderful idea. In working for the Institute, we live and breathe what we are doing. Soon, the success of the program was so incredible that we needed a bigger space, and that's where I think I made my greatest contribution.

We realized that the only way we could afford a new, larger building was to acquire free land. We went to the school board and negotiated a lease of almost four acres for one dollar a year for 50 years, with an option to buy—and succeeded in getting land that is beautifully placed for the Institute. We still lacked money for construction and to begin an endowment. The fundraising went like lightning—we soon reached our goal of raising it all.

The new building turned out to be an incredible facility, contributing to NDI's continuing, tremendous success. Now our concern is having the funds to maintain the building and expand the dance program. We have depended on what we can raise year to year to keep the program going, but many more schools are begging us to bring our program to them. Prospects are good for acquiring public funds to meet NDI's commitment to reach more public schools.

1998 marked four hundred years since the Spanish colonization of New Mexico. The Mayor appointed me to the *Cuartocentenario* Committee overseeing commemorations of that epic colonization. We wanted to remind all the citizens of the state's rich Hispanic history beginning in 1598 as well as honoring the state's history previous to the European colonization. New Mexico's history is unmatched by any other state. Cultural artifacts from the Clovis and Folsom cultures found in New Mexico date back to the earliest human settlement of the continent. Equally impressive is the fact that in New Mexico history stretches from those ancient, stone-age people to cutting-edge scientific research leading to the development of nuclear weapons, their detonation at the Trinity Site, and to the advanced scientific centers at Sandia and Los Alamos National Laboratories and the Santa Fe Institute, all of which are defining the course of modern history.

The main focus of the cuartocentenario was the celebration of 400 years of Spanish settlement. Our activities culminated in the summer of 2003 with the dedication of a bronze monument to the Spanish colonists in a beautiful Santa Fe park. It took nearly three years to renovate the park and complete the monument. As with any attempt at change, the effort wasn't easy, as it came down to a struggle between differing points of view.

The struggle over placement of the cuartocentenario monument was but one of many I've experienced in the course of carrying out group civic endeavors in Santa Fe. Many times discord arises because Santa Fe, although seeming to be a sophisticated, know-it-all city, also harbors many know-nothings. Our groups came up against ill-informed people repeatedly. When we were doing the statue of Santa Fe's founder Peralta, for example, it was generally understood that Peralta would be mounted on a horse. One of the committee—a very snobbish woman, a product of high level art education—declared, "I forbid that we do another statue of a man on a horse. That's absolutely passé. We must have an interpretive monument." She obviously considered the rest of us on the committee as peasants who knew nothing about the new directions public art had taken.

After a long debate, I finally trumped her by putting before her a publication from the Smithsonian Institution that established that the Spanish brought the first modern horses to North America. Many came up the Camino Real with Oñate and Peralta. Prior to that, horses had been extinct in North America for over 10,000 years. In fact, the whole western U.S. horse culture originated with the Hispanic colonization. I put the Smithsonian publication before her and asked her to read aloud. She did so and afterwards all agreed that if there were any man who should be depicted on a horse, it would be Peralta. She shamefacedly surrendered. This incident is but one example of the difficulties that arise with some community leaders in Santa Fe. There exists an ignorance of basic New Mexico history that needs to be confronted.

Santa Fe was founded and functioned for over two centuries as a major center of Spanish administration for a territory almost the size of Europe. It was also at the heart of an epochal colonization, through which Hispanics introduced to the vast western region countless new technologies, domestic animals, agricultural products—a whole new and highly successful culture. I think it's vitally important that New Mexico's citizenry know and appreciate this aspect of our history, which is richer and more wonderful than can be imagined.

Working with civic projects reveals just how many and how diverse are the perceptions of Santa Fe and New Mexico, which may or may not be a good thing. Some hold to a vision of the region as it was in the 1920s, 30s, and 40s, when it was undeveloped and innocent, but sophisticated at the same time, with much activity focused on a revitalization of Native American and Hispanic cultural art forms.

Another vision paints Santa Fe and the northern New Mexico region primarily as a major, lucrative contemporary art center. Others see the state's destiny mainly as a giant tourist attraction, while others believe its greatest assets are its abundant natural resources and its governmental activities, which must be exploited and expanded.

For my part, I see our region as embodying all those visions. I believe, however, that we must always emphasize the state's history and most importantly preserve the incredible, multicultural society that has been created here over the centuries. In this aspect I believe New Mexico is unmatched. We can teach the world how very different cultures can coexist to create an admirable, unique, and viable society.

I worry about the future. Our region faces many pitfalls as well as opportunities. Finding workable solutions to the overriding water problems will require earthshaking decisions. We can't keep growing exponentially just because that's the American way. At some point growth has to be curtailed. The decision to control growth effectively has to be made soon, and it will be wrenching. Perhaps five or ten thousand people in Santa Fe depend on construction for their livelihoods. What would a building moratorium do to them? I see neither the political courage among our leaders nor support from the public to make the dramatic decisions necessary, but eventually we will be forced to act.

Other problems arise because of the attitudes of many of the residents this region now attracts. In the past, probably because it was remote and so different from anywhere else in the U.S., people who moved here were prone to adapt to local ways and to try to become like the local people. Some became more Catholic than the Pope, so to speak. They adjusted to and strongly supported local culture. In fact, people who had moved in from other places founded almost all the important cultural institutions here. It took outsiders to accomplish this because the locals took their cultural treasures for granted. John Gaw Meem, E. Boyd, Alan Vedder, Leonora Paloheimo, Oliver LaFarge and people like them really made a defining difference. Without these extraordinary individuals we'd be much, much poorer.

Unfortunately, many of those moving here now lack that cultural openness. Many come because our region has cachet. Many don't understand the local culture and some don't even want to. In fact, I get the impression that many are repelled by what makes New Mexico unique. Individuals with this attitude make up a growing percentage of the populace. I'm not sure what sort of community we shall have in the future. There is ample reason to be worried and to be challenged to work harder to preserve what we already have achieved.

An unfortunate and bitter event brought home to me this division in the community. For me the experience was reminiscent of front page imbroglios during my Foreign Service career. As a Regent of the Museum of New Mexico, I was enveloped by firestorm over an artistic interpretation of the much-revered Virgin of Guadalupe. In a show of artwork at the Museum of International Folk Art—one of the state's premier cultural institutions—the Virgin was depicted in a flower bikini, supported by a buxom, bare-breasted angel. This statement, created by a militant Chicano lesbian artist, was but one of many examples of interesting new ways of interpreting traditional Hispanic art. However, it was highly offensive to tens of thousands of New Mexicans who deeply revere *la Virgen.*

I had warned the museum's director before the show went up that the Guadalupe work would cause a major uproar, but as if to prove the existence of a deep division between old New Mexico and new New Mexico, I was overruled and the artwork went up. The reaction by tens of thousands of ardent devotees of the Virgin exceeded my worst fears. Within days crowds picketed the museum. The museum's attempt to hold a propitiating meeting were derailed because of hostile participants. Subsequent, lengthy public meetings led to acrimonious debate as those defending artistic freedom argued with those demanding that the artwork, which they considered sacrilegious, be removed. The debacle divided the community as never before, with a most disturbing fracture along ethnic lines adding to the bitterness.

The regents bore the brunt of attacks from both sides. For me it sadly confirmed that large sectors of the community mutually lacked understanding of and even had contempt for the deeply held beliefs of other sectors. I leaned on all my diplomatic skills as I took on a public mediating role, trying to ensure artistic freedom while keeping our public museum clear of needless, divisive and potentially destructive conflict. I suggested a compromise: the artist could either substitute another, less offensive work, exhibit it in a private venue, or she could elect to take the work down earlier than announced. The last of these solutions was the one finally taken.

Noting that the fiercest criticism of the traditional Hispanic viewpoint came from loyal but outraged museum docents, I boldly suggested the museum try harder to incorporate into the docents' ranks some native New Mexicans, who were conspicuously absent. My thanks for this suggestion was a letter on behalf of the docents to the Governor demanding that I be fired. The Governor's office called to assure me that letter went into the wastebasket.

In the uproar over the Lady of Guadalupe exhibit, I once again perceived the very real but most often papered-over divisions in the community. That concerns me very much. (There was additionally, however, a valued plus from this otherwise sad episode. I came to know and work with Dr. Henry Casso, a force of unconditional love, who works unceasingly on the behalf of New Mexico's disadvantaged youth. Working with Dr. Casso to resolve the Guadalupe affair taught me and inspired me much.)

Along with our nation, our community struggles with the crumbling of the family unit. I learned just how precarious the situation is in New Mexico in the course of my work with Think New Mexico. We recognized the importance of starting the education process correctly because our young people lag far behind in so many ways. A structured beginning for kids in an all-day kindergarten, where they could begin to learn to read and interact, would make a difference in their academic achievement and general well being. As we worked toward that end, I was shocked at learning that so many kids come from broken families, with no one watching out for them or urging them on through school. What chance do these kids have, if nobody really cares about them?

As teachers at various schools told us of their kids' dysfunctional home lives, the Think New Mexico board became more convinced than ever that all-day kindergarten would help. After much work,

Think New Mexico reached its goal. Soon all of the kids in the state will attend full-day kindergarten. Knowing that basic learning begins at a very early age, I think New Mexico will next push for pre-kindergarten classes for all.

In my youth, an extended family was the norm. Even a mother with an illegitimate child could count on family to help raise the child as part of a loving group. I especially remember the people of the north, the villagers in Chimayó and Córdova. My nanny, Teófila, was from Córdova. It was my greatest treat to accompany her to Córdova for her vacations. There were so many wonderful, interconnected people there. Now you read about the high percentage of drug addicts in these villages and the high crime rate there. I cannot believe these are the same communities. Many of these terrible problems can be traced to the crumbling of the basic family unit.

In spite of multiple problems, New Mexico is naturally endowed with such great beauty and a still-functional society that it will always be a special place. Many wonderful individuals here appreciate what has been achieved and are willing to expend effort, time, and money to assure that those special qualities are not lost. As things wind down for me, I am confident that the efforts with which I've joined will continue into the future. The organizations to which I have been committed are strong and doing well. Coming back home has been all I wanted it to be.

Postscript

Upon reviewing the draft transcripts of these recollections, I find many painful omissions that make it an incomplete and superficial rendering of my life experiences. But since the story encompasses seventy years of memories, omissions are inevitable. What cannot be permitted is the absence of tribute to a few special, very exceptional individuals that Dolores and I came to know and love.

These people are many and diverse. Egos, personal agendas, deceptions and falseness are common in the official and political world in which I spent a good part of my career, but still we bonded with remarkable human beings. Among the lions, snakes, peacocks, foxes, bulls, worms and weasels, there were eagles and doves that soared above the rest.

Wells Stabler, among my first bosses, mercilessly corrected everything I wrote and challenged everything I did or said. When the time came to overrule the Medical Division of the State Department to admit me as an officer of the Foreign Service, their strict training contributed to my success in overcoming that barrier. Wells remains a very close friend to this day.

My Ethiopian friend, Ghetaneh Haile-Miriam, worked hard to make his country's passage into the modern world a success. He was so intense his palms were always wet, making a handshake a sad experience. When the killings in Ethiopia began he escaped to the U.S.; other dear friends there were not so fortunate.

Bishop Luis Bambaren of Lima, who lived in the slums with the poor, literally radiated goodness. When we visited to say an emotional goodbye, he slipped us shots of potent brandy in delicate demitasse cups to stop our blubbering. Mother Teresa of Calcutta emitted a similar radiance. We came to know her when Dolores helped her establish sanctuaries for the poorest of the poor in Peru and Guatemala. This miniature nun also radiated infinite goodness, which, however, became a little steely when things went awry.

The eleventh Archbishop of Santa Fe, Michael J. Sheehan, was handed his shepherd's crook at a time when his flock was sorely stressed and in danger of scattering. His genuine love for our history and culture and his stalwart, wise leadership has brought the church in New Mexico to the highest levels in nearly all respects in its 400-year history.

In Mexico City, Pilar, the elegant Spanish wife of an English businessman, decided to do something about the horrible conditions in the main maternity hospital, where poor mothers and babies died by the hundreds. Dolores joined her in the delivery rooms and wards, where several mothers shared beds. Dolores and Pilar scrubbed walls and floors, provided clean sheets and bandages, and helped deliver and feed babies. When the Ambassador learned of this, he forbade Dolores and her friends going near the hospital. He feared that our enemies would charge the American women with responsibility for deaths that occurred on their watch. Pilar, abandoned by her American helpers, carried on nonetheless.

In Uruguay, which is home to more kind, decent, honest people than any country I know, we were surrounded with affectionate concern and enveloped by friendship. This warmth and kindness helped us endure the ever-present fear of violence by the Tupamaro terrorists. The legions of wonderful people also made it abundantly obvious that the cruelty of the rebels was an aberration. The situation forced us to send our three oldest children out of the country—a hardship for the whole family—but our Uruguayan friends shared their children with us. In spite of the violence and tension, we have warm memories of Uruguay and the Uruguayans.

Over the years, our family depended very much on a changing cast of household help. Professionals in the Foreign Service and their families often find their health and lives at risk. We relied upon good, trustworthy, loyal help at home to keep the family safe and in good health, allowing Dolores and me to concentrate on our many official obligations. We'll always remember as members of the family Debabe and Leytai in Ethiopia, Francina in Mexico, Benedicta in Peru, Marta in Uruguay, Mr. Parker in Barbados, and Armando and Pedro in Argentina. We might not have made it without them.

In my profession it is usual to deal with the highest strata in government and society, where power is exercised. I knew a couple dozen presidents, a few kings and queens, and hundreds of top officials. President Romeo Lucas García of Guatemala, who had a cobra's eyes and was responsible for thousands of deaths, was my worst burden. President Fernando Belaunde Terry of Peru was an admirable if impractical leader. We bonded with the leadership of many of the countries where we served.

In the U.S. I knew President Truman when he was a senator. Although I only met Presidents Eisenhower and Ford socially, I had direct, official dealings with Presidents Kennedy, Carter, and Reagan. Presidents Johnson and Bush, Sr., I dealt with professionally as well as on a personal basis. My contacts with our various leaders gave me a chance to measure them to my specifications. All were considerate in their dealings with us. Reagan is my odds-on favorite because of his uncluttered, clear, consistent and optimistic vision, which I believe was good for America's people.

I worked directly with Secretaries of State Herter, Rusk, Kissinger, Vance, Christopher and Shultz. They worked me to a frazzle, but we became friends. Kissinger especially has demonstrated his friendship over and over again.

I won't even try to describe my favorite colleagues, who even in a murderously competitive profession, became and remain eternal friends. (However, I reproach myself for not having mentored more young officers as I was mentored.) I shall always miss the late Lt. General Vernon "Dick" Walters, Ambassador to the U.N. and to Germany and a deputy director of the CIA. He was one of nature's most remarkable creations. We bonded with him into a near family relationship.

Finally, I must pay greatest tribute to my companion in all challenges, my helpmate with all burdens, my most acute advisor, the mainstay of not only elaborate official residences but of our intimate family corners. What can I say of the supportive wife, the loving mother, the beautiful person who radiates charm, sincerity and understanding, and who conquers hearts wherever she steps—my Conquistadora, Dolores? Despite the years of professional pressures, all-too-real death threats, bombs, vicious personal attacks, and terror, she never once broke down or added to my problems. I would have accomplished very little without her. After 51 years, we still walk hand in hand into the sunset, accompanied by our children and their families, of whom we are very proud.

As we walk towards that sunset, as if to confirm beyond doubt that I had learned well one of my earliest life lessons, one of our first decisions on returning to Santa Fe was to go to the Rosario Cemetery to assure we had burial plots there. Generations of my ancestors are buried on Rosario's grounds. Not surprised to learn the family plots were chock-a-block full, we managed to find space near the old chapel. We also went to the slightly ghoulish lengths of choosing passages from the sacred scriptures to be inscribed on our tombstones. Perhaps they serve well as an epitaph to this recounting of our lives together.

For Dolores, from the book of Ruth: "For wherever you go I will go, wherever you lodge I will lodge, your people shall be my people and your God my God. Wherever you die I will die, and there be buried."

For me, from Paul's second letter to Timothy: "My life is already being poured away as a libation, and the time has come for me to be gone. I have fought the good fight to the end; I have run the race to the finish; I have kept the faith."

I can imagine Grandmother Alcaria nodding in approval, saying, "*Bien, bien, hijo mío.* (Well done, my son)."